POEMS OF GIOSUÈ CARDUCCI

LECTOR HOUSE PUBLIC DOMAIN WORKS

POEMS OF GIOSUÈ CARDUCCI

GIOSUÈ CARDUCCI,
FRANK SEWALL

ISBN: 978-93-90015-93-1

Published: 1893

LECTOR HOUSE LLP
E-MAIL: lectorpublishing@gmail.com

POEMS OF GIOSUÈ CARDUCCI

TRANSLATED WITH
TWO INTRODUCTORY ESSAYS

I GIOSUÈ CARDUCCI
AND THE HELLENIC REACTION IN ITALY

II CARDUCCI AND THE CLASSIC REALISM

BY

FRANK SEWALL

"Le secret de l'art grec réside là, dans cette finesse à dégager la ligne unique et nécessaire qui évoque la vie et en détermine du coup comme le type éternel"

PAUL BOURGET

1893

PREFACE

In endeavouring to introduce Carducci to English readers through the following essays and translations, I would not be understood as being moved to do so alone by my high estimate of the literary merit of his poems, nor by a desire to advocate any peculiar religious or social principles which they may embody. It is rather because these poems seem to me to afford an unusually interesting example of the survival of ancient religious motives beneath the literature of a people old enough to have passed through a succession of religions; and also because they present a form of realistic literary art which, at this time, when realism is being so perverted and abused, is eminently refreshing, and sure to impart a healthy impetus to the literature of any people. For these reasons I have thought that, even under the garb of very inadequate translations, they would constitute a not unwelcome contribution to contemporary literary study.

I am indebted to the courtesy of Harper & Brothers for the privilege of including here, in an amplified form, the essay on *Giosuè Carducci and the Hellenic Reaction in Italy*, which appeared first in *Harper's Magazine* for July, 1890.

F. S.

WASHINGTON, D. C., June, 1892.

CONTENTS

CONTENTS

vii

ESSAYS

I

GIOSUÈ CARDUCCI AND THE HELLENIC REACTION IN ITALY

The passing of a religion is at once the most interesting and the most tragic theme that can engage the historian. Such a record lays bare what lies inmostly at the heart of a people, and has, consciously or unconsciously, shaped their outward life.

The literature of a time reveals, but rarely describes or analyses, the changes that go on in the popular religious beliefs. It is only in a later age, when the religion itself has become desiccated, its creeds and its forms dried and parcelled for better preservation, that this analysis is made of its passing modes, and these again made the subject of literary treatment.

Few among the existing nations that possess a literature have a history which dates back far enough to embrace these great fundamental changes, such as that from paganism to Christianity, and also a literature that is coeval with those changes. The Hebrew race possess indeed their ancient Scriptures, and with them retain their ancient religious ideas. The Russians and Scandinavians deposed their pagan deities to give place to the White Christ within comparatively recent times, but they can hardly be said to have possessed a literature in the pre-Christian period. Our own saga of Beowulf is indeed a religious war-chant uttering the savage emotions of our Teutonic ancestors, but not a work of literary art calmly reflecting the universal life of the people.

It is only to the Latin nations of Europe, sprung from Hellenic stock and having a continuous literary history covering a period of from two to three thousand years, that we may look for the example of a people undergoing these radical religious changes and preserving meanwhile a living record of them in a contemporaneous literature. Such a nation we find in Italy.

So thorough is the reaction exhibited during the last half of the present century in that country against the dogma and the authority of the Church of Rome that we are led to inquire whether, not the church alone, as Mr. Symonds says,[1] but

[1] "Rome itself had never gathered the Italian cities into what we call a nation; and when Rome, the world's head, fell, the municipalities of Italy remained, and the Italian people sprang to life again by contact with their irrecoverable past. Then, though the church swayed Europe from Italian soil, she had nowhere less devoted subjects than in Italy. Proud as the Italians had been of the empire, proud as they now were of the church, still neither the Roman Empire nor the Roman Church imposed on the Italian character." — *Symonds's*

Christianity itself has ever "imposed on the Italian character" to such an extent as to obliterate wholly the underlying Latin or Hellenic elements, or prevent these from springing again into a predominating influence when the foreign yoke is once removed.

To speak of Christianity coming and going as a mere passing episode in the life of a nation, and taking no deep hold on the national character, is somewhat shocking to the religious ideas which prevail among Christians, but not more so than would have been to a Roman of the time of the Cæsars the suggestion that the Roman Empire might itself one day pass away, a transient phase only in the life of a people whose history was to extend in unbroken line over a period of twenty-five hundred years.

In the work just referred to Mr. Symonds also briefly hints at another idea of profound significance,—namely, whether there is not an underlying basis of primitive race character still extant in the various sections of the Italian people to which may be attributed the variety in the development of art and literature which these exhibit. In his *Studii Letterari* (Bologna, 1880), Carducci has made this idea a fundamental one in his definition of the three elements of Italian literature. These are, he says, the church, chivalry, and the national character. The first or ecclesiastical element is superimposed by the Roman hierarchy, but is not and never was native to the Italian people. It has existed in two forms. The first is Oriental, mystic, and violently opposed to nature and to human instincts and appetites, and hence is designated the ascetic type of Christianity. The other is politic and accommodating, looking to a peaceful meeting-ground between the desires of the body and the demands of the soul, and so between the pagan and the Christian forms of worship. Its aim is to bring into serviceable subjection to the church those elements of human nature or of natural character which could not be crushed out altogether. This element is represented by the church or the ecclesiastical polity. It becomes distinctly Roman, following the eclectic traditions of the ancient empire, which gave the gods of all the conquered provinces a niche in the Pantheon. It transformed the sensual paganism of the Latin races and the natural paganism of the Germanic into a religion which, if not Christianity, could be made to serve the Christian church.

In the same way that the church brought in the Christian element, both in its ascetic and its Roman or semi-pagan form, so did feudalism and the German Empire bring in that of chivalry. This, again, was no native development of the Italian character. It came with the French and German invaders; it played no part in the actions of the Italians on their own soil. "There never was in Italy," says Carducci, "a true chivalry, and therefore there never was a chivalrous poetry." With the departure of a central imperial power the chivalrous tendency disappeared. There remained the third element, that of nationality, the race instinct, resting on the old Roman, and even older Latin, Italic, Etruscan, Hellenic attachments in the heart of the people. Witness during all the Middle Ages, even when the power of the church and the influence of the empire were strongest, the reverence everywhere shown by the Italian people for classical names and traditions. Arnold of Brescia,

"Renaissance in Italy." *Literature.* II., p. 524.

Nicola di Rienzi, spoke to a sentiment deeper and stronger in the hearts of their hearers than any that either pope or emperor could inspire. The story is told of a schoolmaster of the eleventh century, Vilgardo of Ravenna, who saw visions of Virgil, Horace, and Juvenal, and rejoiced in their commendation of his efforts to preserve the ancient literature of the people. The national principle also exists in two forms, the Roman and the Italian—the aulic or learned, and the popular. Besides the traditions of the great days of the republic and of the Cæsars, besides the inheritance of the Greek and Latin classics, there are also the native instincts of the people themselves, which, especially in religion and in art, must play an important part. Arnold of Brescia cried out, "Neither pope nor emperor!" It was then the people, as the third estate, made their voices heard—"*Ci sono anch'io!*" (Here am I too!).

After the elapse of three hundred years from the downfall of the free Italian municipalities and the enslavement of the peninsula under Austrio-Spanish rule, we have witnessed again the achievement by Italians of national independence and national unity. The effect of this political change on the free manifestations of the Italian character would seem to offer another corroboration of Carducci's assertion that "Italy is born and dies with the setting and the rising of the stars of the pope and the emperor." (*Studii Letterari*, p. 44.) Not only with the withdrawal of the Austrian and French interference has the pope's temporal power come to an end, but in a large measure the religious emancipation of Italy from the foreign influences of Christianity in every way has been accomplished. The expulsion of the Jesuits and the secularisation of the schools and of the monastic properties were the means of a more real emancipation of opinion, of belief, and of native impulse, which, free from restraint either ecclesiastical or political, could now resume its ancient habit, lift from the overgrowth of centuries the ancient shrines of popular worship, and invoke again the ancient gods.

The pope remains, indeed, and the Church of Rome fills a large space in the surface life of the people of Italy; and so far as in its gorgeous processions and spectacles, its joyous festivals and picturesque rites, and especially in its sacrificial and vicarious theory of worship, the church has assimilated to itself the most important feature of the ancient pagan religion, it may still be regarded as a thing of the people. But the real underlying antagonism between the ancient national instinct, both religious and civil, and that habit of Christianity which has been imposed upon it, finds its true expression in the strong lines of a sonnet of Carducci's, published in 1871, in the collection entitled *Decennali*. Even through the burdensome guise of a metrical translation, something of the splendid fire of the original can hardly fail to make itself felt. [I]

The movement for the revival of Italian literature may be said to have begun with Alfieri, at the close of the last and the beginning of the present century. It was contemporary with the breaking up of the political institutions of the past in Europe, the dissolution of the Holy Roman Empire, the brief existence of the Italian Republic, the revival for a short joyous moment of the hope of a restored Italian independence. Again a thrill of patriotic ardour stirs the measures of the languid Italian verse. Alfieri writes odes on *America Liberata*, celebrating as the heroes of the new age of liberty Franklin, Lafayette, and Washington. Still more significant of the new life imparted to literature at this time is the sober dignity and strength of Alfieri's sonnets, and the manly passion that speaks in his dramas and marks him as the founder of Italian tragedy.

But the promise of those days was illusory. With the downfall of Napoleon and the return of the Austrian rule, the hope of the Italian nationality again died out. Alfieri was succeeded by Vincenzo Monti and his fellow-classicists, who sought to console a people deprived of future hope with the contemplation of the remote past. This school restored rather than revived the ancient classics. They gave Italians admirable translations of Homer and Virgil, and turned their own poetic writing into the classical form. But they failed to make these dead forms live. These remained in all their beauty like speechless marble exhumed and set up in the light and stared at. If they spoke at all, as they did in the verses of Ugo Foscolo and Leopardi, it was not to utter the joyous emotions, the godlike freedom and delight of living which belonged to the world's youthful time; it was rather to give voice to an all-pervading despair and brooding melancholy, born, it is true, of repeated disappointments and of a very real sense of the vanity of life and the emptiness of great aspirations, whether of the individual or of society. This melancholy, itself repugnant to the primitive Italian nature, opened the way for the still more foreign influence of the romanticists, which tended to the study and love of nature from the subjective or emotional side, and to a more or less morbid dwelling upon the passions and the interior life. With a religion whose life-sap of a genuine faith had been drained away for ages, and a patriotism enervated and poisoned by subserviency to foreign rule and fawning for foreign favour, naught seemed to remain for Italian writers who wished to do something else than moan, but to compose dictionaries and cyclopædias, to prepare editions of the thirteenth-century classics, with elaborate critical annotations, and so to keep the people mindful of the fact that there was once an Italian literature, even if they were to despair of having another. The decay of religious faith made the external forms of papal Christianity seem all the more a cruel mockery to the minds that began now to turn their gaze inward, and to feel what Taine so truly describes as the Puritan melancholy, the subjective sadness which belongs peculiarly to the Teutonic race. The whole literature of the romantic school, whether in Italy or throughout Europe, betrayed a certain morbidness of feeling which, says Carducci, belongs to all periods of transition, and appears alike in Torquato Tasso, under the Catholic reaction of the sixteenth century, and in Châteaubriand, Byron, and Leopardi, in the monarchical restoration of the nineteenth. The despair which furnishes a perpetual undertone to the writing of this school is that which is born of the effort to keep a semblance of life in dead forms of the past, while yet the really living motives of the present have found neither the courage nor the fitting forms for their expression.

In many respects the present revival of Italian literature is a reawakening of the same spirit that constituted the Renaissance of the fourteenth and fifteen centuries, and disappeared under the subsequent influences of the Catholic reaction. Three hundred years of papal supremacy and foreign civic rule have, however, tempered the national spirit, weakened the manhood of the people, and developed a habit of childlike subserviency and effeminate dependence. While restraining the sensuous tendency of pagan religion and pagan art within the channels of the church ritual, Rome has not meanwhile rendered the Italian people more, but, if anything, less spiritual and less susceptible of spiritual teaching than they were in the days of Dante or even of Savonarola. The new Italian renaissance, if we may so name the movement witnessed by the present century for the re-establishment of national unity and the building up of a new Italian literature, lacks the youthful zeal, the fiery ardour which characterised the age of the Medici. The glow is rather that of an Indian summer than that of May. The purpose, the zeal, whatever shall be its final aim, will be the result of reflection and not of youthful impulse. The creature to be awakened and stirred to new life is more than a mere animal; it is a man, whose thinking powers are to be addressed, as well as his sensuous instincts and amatory passion. Such a revival is slow to be set in motion. When once fairly begun, provided it have any really vital principle at bottom, it has much greater promise of permanence than any in the past history of the Italian people. A true renascence of a nation will imply a reform or renewal of not one phase alone of the nation's life, but of all; not only a new political life and a new poetry, but a new art, a new science, and, above all, a new religious faith. The steps to this renewal are necessarily at the beginning oftener of the nature of negation of the old than of assertion of the new. The destroyer and the clearer-away of the débris go before the builder. It will not be strange, therefore, if the present aspect of the new national life of Italy should offer us a number of conspicuous negations rather than any positive new conceptions; that the people's favorite scientist, Mantegazza,—the ultra-materialist,—should be the nation's chosen spokesman to utter in the face of the Vatican its denial of the supernatural; and that Carducci, the nation's foremost and favourite poet, should sing the return of the ancient worship of nature, of beauty, and of sensuous love, and seek to drown the solemn notes of the Christian ritual in a universal jubilant hymn to Bacchus. These are the contradictions exhibited in all great transitions. They will not mislead if the destroyer be not confounded with the builder who is to follow, and the temporary ebullition of pent-up passion be not mistaken for the after-thought of a reflecting, sobered mind. No one has recognized this more truly than Carducci:

> Or destruggiam. Dei secoli
> Lo strato è sul pensiero:
> O pochi e forti, all'opera,
> Chè nei profundi è il vero.
>
> Now we destroy. Of the ages
> The highway is built upon thinking.
> O few and strong, to the work!
> For truth 's at the bottom.

It was in the year 1859, when once more the cry for Italian independence and Italian unity was raised, that the newly awakened nation found its laureate poet in the youthful writer of a battle hymn entitled "Alla Croce Bianca di Savoia"—The White Cross of Savoy. Set to music, it became very popular with the army of the revolutionists, and the title is said to have led to the adoption of the present national emblem for the Italian flag. As a poem it is not remarkable, unless it be for the very conventional commingling of devout, loyal, and valorous expressions, like the following, in the closing stanza:

> Dio ti salvi, o cara insegna,
> Nostro amore e nostra gioja,
> Bianca Croce di Savoja,
> Dio ti salvi, e salvi il Re!

But six years later, in 1865, there appeared at Pistoja a poem over the signature Enotrio Romano, and dated the "year MMDCXVIII from the Foundation of Rome," which revealed in a far more significant manner in what sense its author, Giosuè Carducci, then in his thirtieth year, was to become truly the nation's poet, in giving utterance again to those deeply hidden and long-hushed ideas and emotions which belonged anciently to the people, and which no exotic influence had been able entirely to quench. This poem was called a "Hymn to Satan." The shock it gave to the popular sense of propriety is evident not only from the violence and indignation with which it was handled in the clerical and the conservative journals, one of which called it an "intellectual orgy," but from the number of explanations, more or less apologetic, which the poet and his friends found it necessary to publish. One of these, which appeared over the signature Enotriofilo in the *Italian Athenæum* of January, 1886, has been approvingly quoted by Carducci in his notes to the *Decennali*. We may therefore regard it as embodying ideas which are, at least, not contrary to what the author of the poem intended. From this commentary it appears that we are to look here "not for the poetry of the saints but of the sinners,—of those sinners, that is, who do not steal away into the deserts to hide their own virtues, so that others shall not enjoy them, who are not ashamed of human delights and human comforts, and who refuse none of the paths that lead to these. Not *laudes* or spiritual hymns, but a material hymn is what we shall here find. "Enotrio sings," says his admiring apologist, "and I forget all the curses which the catechism dispenses to the world, the flesh, and the devil. Asceticism here finds no defender and no victim. Man no longer goes fancying among the vague aspirations of the mystics. He respects laws, and wills well, but to him the sensual delights of love and the cup are not sinful, and in these, to him, innocent pleasures Satan dwells. It was to the joys of earth that the rites of the Aryans looked; the same joys were by the Semitic religion either mocked or quenched. But the people did not forget them. As a secretly treasured national inheritance, despite both Christian church and Gothic empire, this ancient worship of nature and of the joys of the earth remains with the people. It is this spirit of nature and of natural sensuous delights, and lastly of natural science, that the poet here addresses as Satan. As Satan it appears in nature's secret powers of healing and magic, in the arts of the sorcerer and of the alchemist. The anchorites, who, drunk with paradise, deprived themselves of the joys of earth, gradually began to listen to these songs from beyond the gratings of their cells—songs of brave deeds, of fair women, and of the triumph of arms. It is Satan who sings, but as they listen they become men again, enamoured of civil glory. New theories arise, new masters, new ideals of life. Genius awakes, and the cowl of the Dominican falls to earth.

Now, liberty itself becomes the tempter. It is the development of human activity, of labour and struggle, that causes the increase of both bread and laughter, riches and honour, and the author of all this new activity is Satan; not Satan bowing his head before hypocritical worshippers, but standing glorious in the sight of those who acknowledge him. This hymn is the result of two streams of inspiration, which soon are united in one, and continue to flow in a peaceful current: the goods of life and genius rebelling against slavery."

With this explanation of its inner meaning we may now refer the reader to the hymn itself. [II]

This poem, while excelled by many others in beauty or in interest, has nowhere, even in the poet's later verses, a rival in daring and novelty of conception, and none serves so well to typify the prominent traits of Carducci as a national poet. We see here the fetters of classic, romantic, and religious tradition thrown off, and the old national, which is in substance a pagan, soul pouring forth in all freedom the sentiments of its nature. It is no longer here the question of either Guelph or Ghibelline; Christianity, whether of the subjective Northern type, brought in by the emperors, or of the extinct formalities of Rome, is bidden to give way to the old Aryan love of nature and the worship of outward beauty and sensuous pleasure. The reaction here witnessed is essentially Hellenic in its delight in objective beauty, its bold assertion of the rightful claims of nature's instincts, its abhorrence of mysticism and of all that religion of introspection and of conscience which the poet includes under the term "Semitic." It will exchange dim cathedrals for the sky filled with joyous sunshine; it will go to nature's processes and laws for its oracles, rather than to the droning priests. While the worship of matter and its known laws, in the form of a kind of apotheosis of science, with which the poem opens and closes, may seem at first glance rather a modern than an ancient idea, it is nevertheless in substance the same conception as that which anciently took form in the myth of Prometheus, in the various Epicurean philosophies, and in the poem of Lucretius. Where, however, Carducci differs from his contemporaries and from the classicists so called is in the utter frankness of his renunciation of Christianity, and the bold bringing to the front of the old underlying Hellenic instincts of the people. That which others wrote about he feels intensely, and sings aloud as the very life of himself and of his nation. That which the foreigner has tried for centuries to crush out, it is the mission of the nation's true poet and prophet to restore.

The sentiments underlying Carducci's writings we find to be chiefly three: a fervent and joyous veneration of the great poets of Greece and Rome; an intense love of nature, amounting to a kind of worship of sunshine and of bodily beauty and sensuous delights; and finally an abhorrence of the supernatural and spiritual elements of religion. Intermingled with the utterances of these sentiments will be found patriotic effusions mostly in the usual vein of aspirants after republican reforms, which, while of a national interest, are not peculiar to the author, and do not serve particularly to illustrate the Hellenistic motive of his writing. The same may be said of his extensive critical labours in prose, his university lectures, his scholarly annotations of the early Italian poets. How far Carducci conforms to the traditional character of the Italian poets—always with the majestic exception of the exiled Dante—in that the soft winds of court favour are a powerful source of their inspiration on national themes, may be judged from the fact that while at the beginning of his public career he was a violent republican, now that he is known to stand high in the esteem and favour of Queen Margherita his democratic utterances have become very greatly moderated, and his praises of the Queen and of the bounties and blessings of her reign are most glowing and fulsome. Without a formal coronation, Carducci occupies the position of poet-laureate of Italy. A little over fifty years of age, an active student and a hard-working professor at the University of Bologna, where his popularity with his students in the lecture-room is equal to that which his public writings have won throughout the land, called from time to time to sojourn in the country with the court, or to lecture before the Queen and her ladies at Rome, withal a man of great simplicity, even to roughness of manners, and of a cordial, genial nature—such is the writer whom the Italians with one voice call their greatest poet, and whom not a few are fain to consider the foremost living poet of Europe.[2]

It would be interesting to trace the development of the Hellenic spirit in the successive productions of Carducci's muse, to note his emancipation from the lingering influences of romanticism, and his casting off the fetters of conventional metre in the *Odi Barbare*. But as all this has been done for us far better in an auto-biographical sketch, which the author gives us in the preface of the *Poesie* (1871), we will here only glance briefly at some of the more characteristic points thus presented.

After alluding to the bitterness and violence for which the Tuscans are famous in their abuse, he informs us that from the first he was charged with an idolatry of antiquity and of form, and with an aristocracy of style. The theatre critics offered to teach him grammar, and the schoolmasters said he was aping the Greeks. One distinguished critic said that his verse revealed "the author's absolute want of all poetic faculty." The first published series of poems was in reality a protest against the religious and intellectual bitterness which prevailed in the decade preceding 1860, "against the nothingness and vanity under whose burden the country was languishing; against the weak coquetries of liberalism which spoiled then as it still spoils our art and our thoughts, ever unsatisfactory to the spirit which will not do things by halves, and which refuses to pay tribute to cowardice." Naturally, even in literary matters inclined to take the opposite side, Carducci felt himself in the majority like a fish out of water. In the revolutionary years 1858 and 1859 he wrote

[2] See *La Poesia e l'Italia nella Quarta Crociata*. Discourses in the presence of her Majesty the Queen. *Nuova Antologia*, Rome, February, 1889.

The poems of Carducci have been published for the most part in the following collections: *Poesie* (Florence, G. Barbera, 1871) comprises the poems previously published under the pseudonym Enotrio Romano in three successive issues—1, *Juvenilia*, the author's early productions in the years 1850-1857, 2, *Levia Gravia*, written between the years 1857 and 1870, and 3, *Decennali*, produced in the decade 1860-1870; *Nuove Poesie*, 1879; *Odi Barbare*, Bologna, 1877; *Nuove Odi Barbare*, 1886; *Nuove Rime*, Bologna, 1887. Besides the last named the publisher Zanichelli, in Bologna, has also issued editions of the author's *Discorsi Letterari e Storici* and *Primi Saggi*; and a complete edition of the author's writings, in twenty vols. 16mo, is promised by the same publisher.

poems on the *Plébiscite* and Unity, counselling the king to throw his crown into the Po, enter Rome as its armed tribune, and there order a national vote. "These," says the poet, "were my worst things, and fortunately were kept unpublished, and so I escaped becoming the poet-laureate of public opinion. In a republic it would have been otherwise. I would have composed the battle pieces with the usual grand words—the ranks in order, arms outstretched in command, brilliant uniforms, and finely curled moustaches. To escape all temptation of this sort I resorted to the cold bath of philosophy, the death-shrouds of learning—*lenzuolo funerario dell'erudizione*. It was pleasant amid all that grand talk of the new life to hide myself in among the cowled shadows of the fourteenth and fifteenth centuries. I journeyed along the Dead Sea of the Middle Ages, studied the movements of revolution in history and in letters; then gradually dawned upon me a fact which at once surprised and comforted me. I found that my own repugnance to the literary and philosophical reaction of 1815 was really in harmony with the experience of many illustrious thinkers and authors. My own sins of paganism had already been committed, and in manifold splendid guises, by many of the noblest minds and geniuses of Europe. This paganism, this cult of form, was naught else but the love of that noble nature from which the solitary Semitic estrangements had alienated hitherto the spirit of man in such bitter opposition. My at first feebly defined sentiment of opposition thus became confirmed conceit, reason, affirmation; the hymn to Phœbus Apollo became the hymn to Satan. Oh, beautiful years from 1861 to 1865, passed in peaceful solitude and quiet study, in the midst of a home where the venerated mother, instead of fostering superstition, taught us to read Alfieri! But as I read the codices of the fourteenth century the ideas of the Renaissance began to appear to me in the gilded initial letters like the eyes of nymphs in the midst of flowers, and between the lines of the spiritual *laude* I detected the Satanic strophe. Meanwhile the image of Dante looked down reproachfully upon me; but I might have answered: 'Father and master, why didst thou bring learning from the cloister into the piazza, from the Latin to the vulgar tongue? Why wast thou willing that the hot breath of thine anger should sweep the heights of papal and imperial power? Thou first, O great public accuser of the Middle Ages, gavest the signal for the rebound of thought: that the alarm was sounded from the bells of a Gothic campanile mattered but little!' So my mind matured in understanding and sentiment to the *Levia Gravia*, and thence more rapidly, in questions of social interest, to the *Decennali*. There are those who complain that I am not what I was twenty-four years ago:—good people, for whom to live and develop is only to feed, like the calf *qui largis invenescit herbis*. In the *Juvenilia* I was the armour-bearer of the classics. In the *Levia Gravia* I held my armed watch. In the *Decennali*, after a few uncertain preliminary strokes of the lance, I venture abroad prepared for every risk and danger. I have read that the poet must give pleasure either to all or to the few; to cater to many is a bad sign. Poetry to-day is useless from not having learned that it has nothing to do with the exigencies of the moment. The lyre of the soul should respond to the echoes of the past, the breathings of the future, the solemn rumours of ages and generations gone by. If, on the contrary, it allows itself to be swayed by the breeze of society's fans or the waving of soldiers' cockades and professors' togas, then woe to the poet! Let the poet express himself and his artistic and moral convictions with the utmost possible candour, sincerity, and courage; as for the rest, it is not his concern. And so it happens that I dare to put forth a book of verses in these days, when one group of our literati are declaring that Italy has never had a language, and another are saying that for some time past we have had no literature; that the fathers do not count for much, and that we are really only in the beginnings. There let them remain; or, as the wind changes, shift from one foreign servitude to another!"

In my selection of poems for translation, regard has been had not so much to the chronological order of their production as to their fitness for illustrating the three important characteristics of Carducci as a national poet which were enumerated above.

The first of these was his strong predilection for the classics, as evinced not only by his veneration for the Greek and Latin poets, but by his frequent attempts at the restoration of the ancient metres in his own verse. Of his fervent admiration for Homer and Virgil let the two sonnets III and IV testify, both taken from the fourth book of the *Levia Gravia*. Already in the *Juvenilia*, during his "classical knighthood," he had produced a poem of some length on Homer, and in the volume which contains the one I have given there are no less than three sonnets addressed to the venerated master, entitled in succession, "Homer," "Homer Again," and "Still Homer." I have chosen the second in order. [III]

In the tribute to Virgil [IV] the beauty of form is only equalled by the tenderness of feeling. It shows to what extent the classic sentiment truly lived again in the writer's soul, and was not a thing of mere intellectual contemplation. In reading it we are bathed in the very air of Campania; we catch a distant glimpse of the sea glistening under the summer moon, and hear the wind sighing through the dark cypresses.

Here it will be proper to notice the efforts made by Carducci not only to restore as to their native soil the long-disused metres of the classic poets, but to break loose from all formal restrictions in giving utterance to the poetic impulse. This intense longing for greater freedom of verse he expresses in the following lines from the *Odi Barbare*:

> I hate the accustomed verse.
> Lazily it falls in with the taste of the crowd,
> And pulseless in its feeble embraces
> Lies down and sleeps.
>
> For me that vigilant strophe
> Which leaps with the plaudits and rhythmic stamp of the chorus,
> Like a bird caught in its flight, which
> Turns and gives battle.

In the preface of the same volume (1877) he pleads in behalf of his new metres that "it may be pardoned in him that he has endeavoured to adapt to new sentiments new metres instead of conforming to the old ones, and that he has thus done for Italian letters what Klopstock did for the Germans, and what Catullus and Horace did in bringing into Latin use the forms of the Eolian lyric."

In the *Nuove Rime* (1887) are three Hellenic Odes, under the titles "Primavere Elleniche," written in three of the ancient metres, the beauty of which would be lost by translation into any language less melodious and sympathetic than the Italian. We give a few lines from each:

I. EOLIA

Lina, brumaio turbido inclina,
Nell'aër gelido monta la sera;
E a me nell'anima fiorisce, O Lina,
La primavera.

II. DORICA

Muorono gli altri dii: di Grecia i numi
Non stanno occaso: ei dormon ne' materni
Tronchi e ne' fiori, sopra i monti, i fiumi,
I mari eterni.

A Cristo in faccia irrigidi nei marmi
Il puro fior di lor bellezze ignude:
Nei carme, O Lina, spira sol nei carme
Lor gioventude.

III. ALESSANDRINA

Lungi, soavi, profondi; Eolia
Cetra non rese più dolci gemiti
Mai nei sì molli spirti
Di Lesbo un dì tra i mirti.

The second of these examples demands translation as exhibiting perhaps more forcibly than any others we could select the boldness with which Carducci asserts the survival of the Hellenic spirit in the love of nature as well as in art and literature, despite the contrary influences of ascetic Christianity:

The other gods may die, but those of Greece
No setting know; they sleep in ancient woods,
In flowers, upon the mountains, and the streams,
And eternal seas.

In face of Christ,[3] in marble hard and firm,
The pure flower of their naked beauty glows;
In songs, O Lina, and alone in songs,
Breathes their endless youth.

The reader is also here referred to the "Invocation." [V]

From this glance at the classic form which is so distinct a feature in Carducci's poems, we proceed to examine the feeling and conceptions which constitute their

[3] Is there an allusion here to Michael Angelo's Christ in the Church of Santa Maria sopra Minerva at Rome?

substance, and which will be found to be no less Hellenic than the metres which clothe them. Nothing could stand in stronger contrast with the melancholy of the romantic school of poets, or with the subjective thoughtfulness and austere introspection of the Christian, than the unfettered outbursts of song in praise of the joy of living, of the delights of love and bodily pleasure, and of the sensuous worship of beautiful form, which we find in the poems "Sun and Love" [VI] and the hymn "To Aurora." [VII]

The latter has in it the freshness and splendour of morning mists rising among the mountains and catching the rosy kisses of the sun. Equally beautiful but full of the tranquillity of evening is the *Ruit Hora* from the *Odi Barbare* of 1877. [VIII]

No one will fail to be struck with the beauty of the figure in the last stanza of this poem, nor with the picturesque force of the "green and silent solitudes" of the first, a near approach to the celebrated and boldly original conception of a *silenzio verde*, a "green silence," which forms one of the many rare and beautiful gems of the sonnet "To the Ox." [IX]

As an example of a purely Homeresque power of description and colouring, and at the same time of an intense sympathy with nature and exquisite responsiveness to every thrill of its life, this sonnet stands at the summit of all that Carducci has written, if indeed it has its rival anywhere in the poetry of our century. The desire to produce in English a suggestion at least of the broad and restful tone given by the metre and rhythm of the original has induced me to attempt a metrical and rhymed translation, even at the inevitable cost of a strict fidelity to the author's every word, and in such a poem to lose a word is to lose much. Nothing but the original can present the sweet, ever-fresh, and sense-reviving picture painted in this truly marvellous sonnet. The unusual and almost grotesque epithet of the opening phrase will be pardoned in view of the singular harmony and fitness of the original.

We know not where else to look for such vivid examples as Carducci affords us of a purely objective and sensuous sympathy with nature, as distinguished from the romantic, reflective mood which nature awakens in the more sentimental school of poets. We feel that this strong and brilliant objectivity is something purely Greek and pagan, as contrasted with the analysis of emotions and thoughts which occupies so large a place in Christian writing. No one is better aware of the existence of this contrast than Carducci himself. For the dear love of nature—that boon of youth before the shadows of anxious care began to darken the mind, or the queryings of philosophy, the conflicts of doubt, and the stings of conscience to torment it—for this happy revelling of mere animal life in the world where the sun shines, the soul of the poet never ceases to yearn and cry out. The consciousness of the opposite, of a world of thought, of care, and of conscience ever frowning in sheer stern contrast from the strongholds of the present life and the opinions of men—this is what introduces a kind of tragic motive into many of these poems, and adds greatly to their moral, that is, their human interest. For the poetry of mere animal life, if such were poetry, however blissful the life it describes, would still not be interesting.

Something of this pathos appears in the poem "To Phœbus Apollo," [X] where the struggle of the ancient with the present sentiments of the human soul is depicted. It will interest the reader to know that at the time this poem was written (it appeared in Book II. of the *Juvenilia*) the author had not broken so entirely with the conventional thought of his time and people but that he could consent to write a *lauda spirituale* [XI] for a procession of the *Corpus Domini*, and a hymn for the Feast of the Blessed Diana Guintini, protectress of Santa Maria a Monti in the lower Valdarno. When called by the *Unità Cattolica* to account for this sudden transformation of the hymn-writer into the odist of Phœbus Apollo, Carducci replied by reminding his clerical critics that even in his nineteenth year he was given to writing parodies of sacred hymns, and he further offers by way of very doubtful apology the explanation that, being invited by certain priests who knew of his rhyming ability to compose verses for their feasts, the thought came into his head, "being in those days deeply interested in Horace and the thirteenth-century writers, to show that faith does not affect the *form* of poetry, and that therefore without any faith at all one might reproduce entirely the forms of the blessed laudists of the thirteenth century. I undertook the task as if it were a wager."

In the lines of the poem *To Phœbus Apollo* there is traceable a romantic melancholy, the faint remnant of the impression left by those writers through whom, says Carducci, "I mounted to the ancients, and dwelt with Dante and Petrarch," viz., Alfieri, Parini, Monti, Foscolo, and Leopardi. He has not yet broken entirely with subjective reflection and its gloom, and entrusted himself to the life which the senses realize at the present moment as the whole of human well-being. This sentiment becomes more strongly pronounced in the later poems, where not even a regret for the past is allowed to enter to distract the worship of the present, radiant with its divine splendour and bounty. The one thought that can cast a shadow is the thought of death; but this is not at all to be identified with Christian seriousness in reflecting on the world to come. The poet's fear of death is not that of a judgment, or a punishment for sins here committed, and hence it is not associated with any idea of the responsibility of the present hour, or of the amending of life and character in the present conduct. The only fear of death here depicted is a horror of the absence of life, and hence of the absence of the delights of life. It is the fear of a vast dreary vacuum, of cold, of darkness, of nothingness. The moral effect of such a fear is only that of enhancing the value of the sensual joys of the present life, the use of the body for the utmost of pleasure that can be got by means of it. This more than pagan materialism finds its bold expression in the lines from the *Nuove Odi Barbare* entitled "Outside the Certosa." [XII]

In studying the religious or theological tendency of Carducci's muse, it is necessary to bear in mind constantly the inherent national blindness of the Hellenic and, in equal if not greater degree, the Latin mind to what we may call a spiritual conception of life, its duties, and its destiny. But in addition to this blindness towards the spiritual elements or substance of Christianity there is felt in every renascent Hellenic instinct a violent and unrelenting hostility towards that ascetic form and practice which, although in no true sense Christian, the greater religious orders and the general discipline of the Roman Church have succeeded in compelling Christianity to wear. The mortification of nature, the condemnation of all worldly and corporeal delights, not in their abuse, but in their essential and orderly use, the dishonouring of the body in regarding its beauty as only an incentive to sin, and in making a virtue of ugliness, squalor, and physical weakness—these things have the offensiveness of deadly sins to the sensuous consciousness of minds of the Hellenic type. To spiritual Christianity Carducci is not adverse because it is spiritual—as such it is still comparatively an unknown element to Italian minds—but because it is foreign to the national instinct; because it came in with the emperors, and so it is indissolubly associated with foreign rule and oppression. It is the Gothic or Teutonic infusion in the Italian people that has kept alive whatever there is of spiritual life in the Christianity that has been imposed on them by the Roman Church. The other elements of Romanism are only a sensuous cult of beautiful and imposing forms in ritual, music, and architecture on the one hand; and on the other a stern, uncompromising asceticism, which in spirit is the direct contradiction of the former. While the principle of asceticism was maintained in theory, the sincerity of its votaries gradually came to be believed in by no one; the only phase of the church that seized hold of the sympathies and affections of the people was the pagan element in its worship and its festivals; and seeing these, the popes were wise enough to foster this spirit and cater in the most liberal measure to its indulgence, as the surest means of maintaining their hold on the popular devotion. In the ever-widening antagonism between the spirit and the flesh, between the subjective conception of Christianity on the one hand, as represented by the Teutonic race and the empire, and the sensuous and objective on the other, as represented by the Italic race and the pope, may we not discern the reason why the Italian people, in the lowest depths of their sensual corruption, were largely and powerfully Guelph in their sympathies, and why the exiled and lonely writer of the *Divina Commedia* was a Ghibelline? It is at least in the antagonism of principles as essentially native *versus* foreign that we must find the explanation of the cooling of Carducci's ardour towards the revered master of his early muse, even while the old spell of the latter is still felt to be as irresistible as ever. This double attitude of reverence and aversion we have already seen neatly portrayed in the reference Carducci makes in the autobiographical notes given above to Dante as the great "accuser of the Middle Ages who first sounded the signal for the reaction of modern thought," with the added remark that the signal being sounded from a "Gothic campanile" detracted but little from the grandeur of its import. The same contrast of sentiment finds more distinct expression in the sonnet on Dante in Book IV. of the *Levia Gravia*. [XIII]

But nowhere is the contrast between the Christian sense of awe in the presence of the invisible and supernatural and the Hellenic worship of immediate beauty and sensuous pleasure displayed in such bold and majestic imagery as in the poem entitled "In a Gothic Church." [XIV] Here, in the most abrupt and irreverent but entirely frank transition from the impression of the dim and lofty cathedral nave to the passion kindled by the step of the approaching loved one, and in the epithets of strong aversion applied to the holiest of all objects of Christian reverence, the very shock given to Christian feeling and the suddenness of the awful descent from heavenly to satyric vision tell, with the prophetic veracity and power of true poetry, what a vast chasm still unbridged exists between the ancient inherent Hellenism of the Italian people and that foreign influence, named indifferently by Carducci Semitic or Gothic, which for eighteen centuries has been imposed without itself imposing on them.

The true poet of the people lays bare the people's heart. If Carducci be, indeed, the national poet of Italy we have in this poem not only the heart but the religious sense—we had almost said the conscience—of the Italian people revealed to view. Nor is this all Bacchantic; the infusion of the Teutonic blood in the old Etruscan and Italic stock has brought the dim shadows of the cathedral and its awful, ever-present image of the penalty of sin to interrupt the free play of Italian sunshine. But just as on the canvas of the religious painters of the Renaissance angels as amorous Cupids hover about between Madonna and saints, and as in the ordinary music of an Italian church the organist plays tripping dance melodies or languishing serenades between the intoned prayers of the priests or the *canto firmo* psalms of the choir, so here we behold the sacred aisles of the cathedral suddenly invaded by the dancing satyr, who, escaping from his native woods, has wandered innocently enough into this his ancient but strangely disguised shrine.

The stanzas that follow describe Dante's vision of the "Tuscan Virgin" rising transfigured amid the hymns of angels. The poet, on the contrary, sees neither angels nor demons, but is conscious only of feeling

> The cold twilight
> To be tedious to the soul,

and then exclaims:

> Farewell, Semitic God: the mistress Death
> May still continue in thy solemn rites,
> O far-off king of spirits, whose dim shrines
> Shut out the sun.

> Crucified Martyr! Man thou crucifiest;
> The very air thou darkenest with thy gloom.
> Outside, the heavens shine, the fields are laughing,
> And flash with love.

> The eyes of Lidia—O Lidia, I would see thee
> Among the chorus of white shining virgins
> That dance around the altar of Apollo
> In the rosy twilight,

> Gleaming as Parian marble among the laurels,
> Flinging the sweet anemones from thy hand,
> Joy from thy eyes, and from thy lips the song
> Of a Bacchante!

ODI BARBARE.

Notwithstanding the bold assertion of the Hellenic spirit in this and in the greater part of his poems, that, nevertheless, Carducci has not been able to restore his fair god of light and beauty, the Phœbus Apollo, to the undisputed sway he held in the ancient mind is evident from the shadows of doubt, of fear, and anxious questioning which still darken here and there the poet's lines, as in the sonnet *Innanzi, Innanzi!* [XV] It is here that the stern element of tragedy, the real tragedy of humanity, makes itself felt in this rhapsodist of joy and of love. It comes to tell us that to the Italian as he is to-day life has ceased to be a carnival, and that other sounds than that of the Bacchante's hymn have gained an entrance, with all their grating discord, to his ear: and to silence this intruder will the praises of Lidia and of Apollo suffice, be they sung on a lyre never so harmonious and sweet? In this sonnet is depicted in wonderful imagery the ancient and awful struggle which the sensuous present life sustains with the question of an eternity lying beyond.

While our interest in Carducci is largely owing to the character he bears as the poet of the Italian people, it would be quite erroneous to consider him a popular poet. For popularity, whether with the court, the school, or the masses, he never aimed, as is evident from his satisfaction at narrowly escaping being made a political poet-laureate. Instead of writing down to the level of popular apprehension and taste, he rather places himself hopelessly aloof from the contact of the masses by his style of writing, which, simple and pure as it seems to the cultured reader, is nevertheless branded by the average Italian as learned and obscure, and not suited to the ordinary intelligence. As an innovator both in the form and in the content of his verse, he has still a tedious warfare to wage with a people so conservative as the Italians of old habits and old tastes, confirmed as these have been by the combined influence of centuries of political and ecclesiastical bondage. But Carducci's writing, springing nevertheless from a strong instinct, looks only to the people for a final recognition, even though that has to be obtained through the medium of the learned classes at first. How far he has succeeded in getting this vantage-ground of a general recognition and acquiescence on the part of the learned, the following testimony from Enrico Panzacchi, himself a critic and a poet of high reputation, may help us to conclude:

"I believe that I do not exaggerate the importance of Carducci when I affirm that to him and to his perseverance and steadfast courageous work we owe in great part the poetic revival in Italy.

"I have great faith, I confess, in the initiative power of men of strong genius and will, and, to tell the truth, while it is the fashion of the day to explain always the individual by the age he lived in, I think it is often necessary to invert the rule, and explain the age by the individual."

He goes on to show that, indifferent alike to conventional laws and public opinion, Carducci always persisted in the constant endeavour to *far l'arte*, to "do his art." He defied the critics, and tried to be himself.

Mr. Symonds says of the Renaissance that "it was a return in all sincerity and faith to the glory and gladness of nature, whether in the world without or in the soul of man." Carducci reflects the spirit of the Renaissance in so far as by setting free the national instincts he has made way for the Hellenic reaction in favour of the "glory and the gladness of the world without." He has shown, moreover, how foreign to these instincts is Christianity, considered apart from the Roman Church, whether in its ascetic or in its spiritual aspects. But it cannot be said of him, whatever may have been true of the poets of the Renaissance, that he has reawakened or rediscovered "the glory and gladness of nature in the soul of man," and without this the gladness of the world without is but a film of sunshine hiding the darkness of the abyss. Indeed, if the soul and not the senses be addressed, we question whether beneath all the Dionysian splendours and jollity of Carducci's verses there be not discernible a gloom more real than that of Leopardi. Even for Italy the day is past when Hellenism can fill the place of Christianity; the soul craves a substance for which mere beauty of form, whether in intellect, art, or nature, is a poor and hollow substitute; and to revive not the poetry alone, but the humanity of the nation, a force is needed greater and higher than that to be got by the restoration of either dead Pan or Apollo.

II

CARDUCCI AND THE CLASSIC REALISM

Sojourning one autumn in a quiet *pension* at Lugano, I came in contact with a fellow-boarder, who, notwithstanding he bore the title of a Sicilian count of very high-sounding name, proved on acquaintance to be a man of serious literary taste and not above accepting pecuniary compensation for the products of his pen.

He was engaged at that time in translating into the Italian a well-known English classic, and was in the habit of appealing to me occasionally for my judgment as to the accuracy of his interpretation of an English word or phrase.

This led to pleasant interviews on the literary art in general.

It was one day when the conversation turned on the extreme materialism of certain scientific writers of the day, and especially on Mantegazza of Florence, whose grossness in treating of the human passions has called forth expressions of disgust from Italians, as well as others, that my Sicilian friend quietly remarked, "We Italians can never allow the holy Trine to be destroyed—the True, the Good, the Beautiful. It is not enough that a writer tell the facts as they are; nor that his purpose be a useful one; there must be the element of beauty also in his work, or the Italians will not accept it; and the ugly, the monstrous, and deformed the Italians will not endure."

I thought herein he proved his lineage from a stock older than even his family title—that old race of the land where Theocritus sang as if for beauty alone, and whose Ætna cherishes still her deep-down fires uncooled and untamed by modern as by ancient contrivances of man.

It is this presence of the love of the beautiful that everywhere accompanies the Greek race and their descendants, and imparts what we may call the Hellenic instinct of form. And in this sense of form born of the love of beauty lies the secret of the immortal art of the Greeks, whether as presented in sculpture, architecture, painting, or letters.

The survival of a certain Hellenic religious feeling in the Italian people after centuries of a superimposed Christianity has already been treated of in the previous essay. I desire here to speak of Carducci as affording an example—perhaps one among many, but I know none better—of the restoration of the Greek love of form to modern letters, and so as illustrating what we may designate as the classic realism.

No term has been more abused of late years than this word—realism. Become the watchword of schools of "realists" in every branch of art and literature, it has been reduced at last to a service as empty of meaning as was ever the vaguest idealism empty of reality.

The tendency of the age has been unquestionably one of ultimation; everything presses into the plane of outermost effect. We have seemed to be no more satisfied with the contemplation of intangible ideals: we rest content only with what hand can touch and eye rest upon. The "power in ultimates" is the display of force characteristic of this age of the world. The forces physical and mental have been always there: it has taken a time like the present, an age of inventive frenzy filled with a yearning for the doing and trying of things long dreamt of, to give vent to these hidden forces.

This tendency to ultimation, the seeking expression of inmost emotions and conceptions in material embodiments, has characterized of late years every form of mental activity.

Religion exemplifies it in the impatience the people exhibit at fine analyses of doctrines and laborious attempts at creed-patching, at the same time that they are ready to engage in schemes of benevolence and social reform unparalleled in the history of the past. They would fain substitute a religion of doing for a religion of believing; and so impatient are they of the restrictions of dogma that they resent inquiry into the quality or inward motive of the doing, or even into its moral effect in the long run, so only some "good work" be done and done quickly.

We see the same tendency in music and the drama wonderfully illustrated in the whole conception and effort of the Wagnerian school. Expression is everything. The question is not—Is the thing in itself noble, but is the expression of it complete, unhindered by previous conventionalities? Is nothing kept back, or left to the imagination, but everything, rather, brought out into the actuality of sound, of color, of living performers, and material accessories?

The Ibsen drama, the Tourguenief and Tolstoi school of novelists, not to speak of Zola and his followers in France, writers like Capuana and Verga in Italy, and, although in a quite different vein, Howells among novelists and Whitman among poets in America, have aimed chiefly to give a faithful account of life as it is seen. Some have come dangerously near the assertion that by some mysterious law the bold doing ennobles even a commonplace motive, and that a regard for truth is enough whether there be any beauty behind it or not.

The power realised in full and free expression is one of the most exquisite delights known to man. We of a northern race who, according to the saying of our French neighbor, "take our pleasures sadly," do so because of a hereditary conviction of the sanctity of the unexpressed. We have therefore been slowest in arriving at these efforts towards realism, or the untrammelled giving forth of the inward self into outward embodiment. That pure externalism of the southern or Greek nature which sought its highest satisfaction in a visible embodiment of the divine in art, and which distinguishes still the Roman from the Saxon religious nature, has been regarded as verging on the sinful. It is not strange that a tendency so long suppressed when once set free should rush even into lawless extremes, and that an age or school of writers tasting the delights of this liberty for the first time should be loth to resign it and be ready rather to sacrifice all to its further extension. It is quite in accordance with this theory that puritan America should have given birth to Walt Whitman, who, with all his lawlessness, is in many respects the most of a Greek that modern literature can show.

To what extremes this delight has sought indulgence is shown not more plainly in Zola and his school above mentioned than in the whole contemporary school of French pictorial art. We see here how form, as expression, indulged in for its own sake, apart from a due consideration of the substance within the form, becomes itself monstrous and vicious. This is the essentially *immoral* element in art—the licentious worship of form, or of external shape, regardless of an internal soul or motive.

When the realist says: "With the motive of nature, of society, of man, I have nothing to do; it is enough if I portray faithfully his conduct," he thereby advertises the fact that he is not an artist, but a kind of moral photographer. He falls short of being an artist in just the degree in which he sees the details of form apart from their soul or spiritual essence; and as this spiritual element is that wherein the unity of the world as idea exists, therefore, failing to apprehend this, he fails to lay hold of the universal aspects which alone can assign true relation and true meaning to any of the details treated of. It is the apprehension of the universal element underlying the particulars that constitutes the peculiar gift of the artist. It is indeed true that nature, or humanity, is its own interpreter and its own preacher; and the most faithful servant of either will be he who most exactly presents his subject as he finds it. But the subject is never found by the true artist detached from its community-life, or severed from the endless woof of combinations, of causes and effects, of law and recompense, which go to make up any present moment of its existence; these constitute its "story." So far as these inner conditions are recognized and felt in giving the ultimate expression, so far alone is the portrayal a real one in the true sense.

Undoubtedly the inmost motive that can give form to the literature of any age or race is the religious one, by which I mean the recognition of a life within and above nature, not our own, but to which we entertain a personal relation. This is in the truest sense that "soul" which "is form, and doth the body make," and its presence or absence is what sufficiently distinguishes the true from a false realism.

An age without a religion can produce only a soulless, and so an unreal, art. What it calls art may abound in shape, but will possess no form in the true sense of the word. For form is the combination of particulars with a view to a single purpose, for which every particular exists and to which it is subordinate; it is therefore never a many, but always a one out of many. This inward controlling motive that constitutes out of many the one, is the living substance within every true or real form. That which does not possess this motive of unity is not form, but shape, or an artificial cast made to resemble the living thing, but having no life within it. Art is thus the form that grows from within, while shape is but the impression mechanically imposed on passive and lifeless material from without. The modern French school of realists in art are the fittest examples of this substitution of shape for form, and so of pseudo-realism. They have given us corpses, whether physical or moral, and called them human beings. They have preferred the charnel-house, the dissecting-room, or the field of carnage, as the subjects in which to display most effectively their realism. The more revolting the subject, the more hideously exact the representation, the more credit was claimed for the artist. In literature the case was parallel. Nothing so vile but it was to be admired for its faithfulness in representation. The inner motive, the moral purpose of the writing or the painting, was not only not there, but the producer scorned the judgment that would look for it. Never was religion, or the sentiment of reverence for the spiritual as the world's idea, so manifestly wanting as in these recent French materialists. The abjuring of the romantic and the ideal has gone so far as to extinguish the human element, and so we find in these schools skilfully painted bodies and an almost matchless power of expression; but, after all, how little is expressed!

Compare a Greek statue of Phidias's time with the latest production of a Parisian studio. Both are alike of hard, colourless, senseless marble; but can we not see in one the breathing of a god, while in the other we, at the most, study with a critical vision the outlines of a human animal?

Reality is not reached by the negative process of taking away conventional guises and concealments; and yet modern artists and writers have alike thought to get at truth in this way. But the nude is not the more real for being nude. The reality of an object depends on what is within it, and not on anything that men put on or take away from it. How many writers of late years have been deluding themselves with the idea that if one can only succeed in avoiding everything like a moral purpose, or even interesting situations, and reveal what they call the bare facts of experience, one may thereby attain to the real? As if ever art existed except in the discovering of unity, the interpretation of purpose, and in the suggesting of that which is interesting to the human heart!

The emptiness of this kind of realism, which is as naked of soul within as of garments without, is proved by the reaction that is already setting in in France, where materialism has made its boldest claims in the domain of art. Not only in art is there a strong movement for restoring the lost elements of romance and piety, leading to a religious severity almost like that of the pre-Raphaelites, but in literature there is a similar protest against the degradation of the real to the plane of mere soulless matter. M. Paul Bourget, who has been through all phases of French expression and knows its extremes, gives voice to this reaction in the following passage from his "Sensations d'Italie":

"Sans doute, les grands peintres ont vu d'abord et avant tout l'être vivant; mais dans cet être, ils ont dégagé la *race* et ils ne pouvaient pas la sentir, cette race, sans démêler l'obscur idéal qui s'agite en elle, qui végète dans les créatures inférieures, ignoré d'elles-mêmes et cependant consubstantiel à leur sang. La langueur et la robustesse à la fois de ce pays de montagnes dont le pied baigne dans la fièvre, le mysticisme des compatriotes de Saint François d'Assise et leur sauvagerie, la mélancolie songeuse prise devant l'immobile sommeil des lacs, tous ces traits élaborés par le travail séculaire de l'hérédité, le Pérugin les a dégagés plus nettement qu'un autre, mais it n'a eu qu'à les dégager. Sa divination instinctive les a reconnus, sans peut-être qu'il s'en rendît compte, dans des coupes de joues, des nuances de prunelles, des airs de tête. C'est là, dans cette interprétation à la fois soumise et géniale, que réside la véritable copie de la nature où tout est âme, même et surtout la forme,—âme qui se cherche, qui se méconnaît parfois, qui s'avilit, mais une âme tout de même et qui ne se révèle qu'à l'âme."[4]

A Frenchman of to-day become an admirer of Perugino!

A tendency to realism, unlike that of French art in subject, but not unlike in method, is that which is exhibited in England in the recent religious novelists of the class headed by the authoress of "Robert Elsmere." Here, again, the effort has been to get at the real by stripping off conventional religious admissions, pretensions, and errors, and depicting a moral basis of conduct which can exist independently of creed and church. The result has been disappointing, because a creed incapable of perversion or corruption becomes as lifeless and as powerless a factor in human character-building as is the multiplication table; and without a miraculous incarnation of Deity as its basis and its imperative authority, the whole system of Christian ethics, when thus reduced to a scientific conclusion or to an invention of man's individual moral sense, loses not only its power to influence morally, but even to interest other minds. The "real" basis of religion thus arrived at is found to be no religion at all, but only the private opinion of this authoress as to what is good and right, with every divine and therefore every universal and obligatory element in it left out.

I have spoken indiscriminately, above, of the realists in our modern literature as all subject to the temptation to rest satisfied with photographic imitations of nature rather than with a reality created from their apprehension of its ideal form. The end sought for is faithfulness in expression, and the danger is that of making subordinate to this the substance of what is expressed. But among these writers there are all degrees of approach to the genuine realism which undoubtedly, like the art of the Greeks, is a thing that can never die, and which, even if for a long interval set aside, is sure to return again to its rightful place as the only true form of expression.

Among the various aspirants to the title of realist, we have no more interesting examples than in our own Howells and Whitman, both being avowed prophets of this school of writing. In Whitman we see a generous nature run away with by the

---

[4] "Doubtless the great painters saw, first and before all things, the human being; but in this being they saw the race, and they could not discern the race without disengaging the vague ideal which struggles in it, which exists even in inferior creatures, unknown to themselves and yet consubstantial with their blood. The languor and, at the same time, the strength of this land of mountains, whose feet are bathed by the waters of fever-breeding marshes, the mysticism and the wildness of the compatriots of St. Francis of Assisi, the dreamy melancholy inspired by the contemplation of sleeping lakes—all those traits, elaborated by the working of heredity through centuries, Perugino saw more clearly than any one else, but he had only to detect them. He divined them instinctively in the outline of the cheek, the colour of the eye, the turn of the head. It is in this interpretation, at once humble and sympathetic, that the veritable imitation of nature consists, in which all is soul, even, and above all the form—a soul which seeks itself, disguises itself at times and even debases itself, but a soul nevertheless and one that reveals itself only to the soul."

passion of expression. His words are heaped like sand-dunes. There is a sound of roaring waves, but the landscape is, too often, on the whole, shapeless and wearisome. One feels that there is meaning in the poet's mind, but the expression is excessive, and so without form. The delight of ultimation has become a frenzy of word-piling or word-inventing. The disappointment is like that experienced on seeing a piece of sculpture which reveals a bold and vigorous design with magnificent anatomy and muscular strength, but which has a weak line in the face. It just falls short of being art.

With Howells the charm of his realism lies in the subtlety of his concealment of it. The deep moral purpose which, like a strong, irresistible current, underlies his recent and more serious writing, is all the more potent because it is not "pointed"; and the reader is allowed to indulge, as if with the author himself, in the little delusion that this is only the ordinary superficial aspect of an every-day world which is being described, and that things do thus merely happen as they happen, without design or reason. So perfect is the form and so true to nature that, with the author, we keep up, too, the little deception, that it is with the form itself that we are pleased, and that this constitutes the realism of which the author is so ardent an advocate. Meanwhile we learn, when the story is ended, that this realism was all informed with a soul of moral and divine purpose, and that this is all that is real in it as in anything else.

To distinguish from the pseudo-realism of matter the genuine realism that is soul-informed, I do not know a better name for the latter than the Classic Realism. I mean by this something as far remote as possible from the classic formalism of the age of Pope and Dryden, as remote indeed as form is from formalism. For in that period it was neither truth to nature nor truth to the imagination that was aimed at in expression, but rather a cold and rigid conformity to the rules of correct writing as found in the recognized standards. "Classic" hence got to mean merely according to the standards. But by a Classic Realism we will certainly understand that effort to obtain a form of expression which recognizes both the internal and the external reality of things, and is able to combine both in one ultimation like the soul and body that make the one man.

The subjectivity of the Saxon mind and a large inheritance of both the classic formalism and the romanticism of former periods of English literature have prevented our English writers from attaining that spontaneous realism which was native to the Hellenic mind; and yet they have the gift to recognise and interpret it when found. This did Tennyson when he chose for translation the following lines closing the Eighth Book of the "Iliad":

> As when in heaven the stars about the moon
> Look beautiful, when all the winds are laid,
> And every height comes out, and jutting peak,
> And valley, and the immeasurable heavens
> Break open to their highest; and all the stars
> Shine, and the shepherd gladdens in his heart:
> So, many a fire between the ships and stream
> Of Xanthus blazed before the towers of Troy,

A thousand on the plain: and close by each
Sat fifty in the blaze of burning fire;
And, champing golden grain, the horses stood,
Hard by their chariots, waiting for the dawn.

The same vision into the charmed world of the classic realism had Keats when he wrote his sonnet "On First Looking into Chapman's Homer," and put a whole age of ecstatic delight into these matchless lines:

Oft of one wide expanse had I been told
That deep-browed Homer ruled as his demesne:
Yet did I never breathe its pure serene
Till I heard Chapman speak out loud and bold:
Then felt I like some watcher of the skies
When a new planet swims into his ken;
Or like stout Cortez when, with eagle eyes,
He stared at the Pacific—and all his men
Look'd at each other with a wild surmise—
Silent, upon a peak in Darien.

Listen to Theocritus describing in most realistic language the Joys of Peace. Notice how he does not so much as mention any emotion, but awakens it by his faithful description of the objective world:

And oh! that they might till rich fields, and that unnumbered sheep and fat might bleat cheerily through the plains, and that oxen, coming in herds to the stalls, should urge on the traveller by twilight. And oh! that the fallow lands might be broken up for sowing, when the cicada, sitting on his tree, watches the shepherd in the open day and chirps on the topmost spray; that spiders may draw their fine webs over martial arms, and not even the name of the battle-cry be heard. [Idyl XVI.]

Keats has felt the same appeal of nature to human sympathy in all the humblest forms of life, and has expressed it in his sonnet on the "Grasshopper and the Cricket":

The poetry of earth is never dead.
When all the birds are faint with the hot sun,
And hide in cooling trees, a voice will run
From hedge to hedge about the new-mown mead:
That is the grasshopper's—he takes the lead
In summer luxury—he has never done
With his delights, for, when tired out with fun,
He rests at ease beneath some pleasant weed.
The poetry of earth is ceasing never:
On a lone winter evening, when the frost
Has wrought a silence, from the stove there shrills
The cricket's song, in warmth increasing ever,
And seems to one in drowsiness half lost,

The grasshopper's among some grassy hills.

This is realism, but a truly classic realism; it is earth, but the "poetry of earth."

Probably Whitman has here and there approached as nearly as any English writer to this pure realism, and, when he has not allowed his delight in words to outrun his inward conception, he has given us pictures possessing much of the vivid objectivity of the Greek realists. Compare with the above passage from Theocritus the Farm Picture drawn by Whitman in these two lines:

Through the ample open door of the peaceful country barn
A sun-lit pasture field, with cattle and horses feeding.

Or this:

Lo, 'tis autumn.
Lo, where the trees, deeper green, yellower and redder,
Cool and sweeten Ohio's villages, with leaves fluttering in the moderate wind,
Where apples ripe in the orchards hang and grapes on the trellis'd vines,
(Smell you the smell of the grapes on the vines?
Smell you the buckwheat where the bees were lately buzzing?)
Above all, lo, the sky so calm, so transparent after the rain, and with wondrous clouds,
Below, too, all calm, all vital and beautiful, and the farm prospers well.

Perhaps it is because Whitman is not the literary heir of the past, but the beginner of his line, that he enjoys this freedom and completeness of ultimation. He could dare what Keats, born to the purple, would fain have dared, but, in his sonnet to Haydon, confesses his fear of attempting:

Haydon! forgive me that I cannot speak
Definitively of these mighty things;
Forgive me that I have not eagles' wings,
That what I want I know not where to seek.
And think that I would not be over meek
In rolling out up-followed thunderings
Even to the steep of Heliconian springs,
Were I of ample strength for such a freak.

Undoubtedly true it is that a spring-like freshness and vigour in Whitman's poems give voice to the life of a strong and youthful nationality; and in grateful appreciation of this we will not stop to inquire to what extent he owes his present popularity to the charm of novelty. But, novel as his style may seem, it is but the re-discovered secret of all true art, the realism that is the ultimation of the soul.

That Goethe was a realist in this sense is shown by the fact that where the emotion was deepest and the moral substance of his writing the most intense and unmistakable, the form was purely objective and classic—dealing with the simplest and commonest of the world's every-day material, and indulging in little or no reflection or introspection. Such is he in the *Hermann und Dorothea*, at once the most Teutonic and the most Hellenic of modern poems. Of this Professor Dowden says in a recent essay:[5]

"Goethe never attempted to transform himself into a Greek; on the contrary, it seemed to him essential for the object which he had in view that he should remain a German, since it was from the alliance of the Teutonic genius with the genius of Greece that he hoped for the birth of the ardent child Euphorion. And in the representative poem of this period, *Hermann und Dorothea,* if Goethe is more than elsewhere a Greek in the bright purity of his art and its fine simplicity of outline, here also more than elsewhere in the body of thought and feeling he is a German of the Germans."

Coming now to study Carducci as a poet who more perfectly than any other living, perhaps, reflects the classic realism of his Hellenic literary ancestry, I desire to emphasise as a point of peculiar interest the fact that the religious element which I have spoken of above as the most essential one in all art is here not Christian, but avowedly pagan; but that, as such, it supplies that inward essence to Carducci's poems that gives them reality. There is all the difference imaginable between the description of landscape in his poem on the peninsula of Sermione [XVI] and that of our modern writers who think to have outgrown Christianity and see no suggestion of supernatural presence or influence in the world around them. Were Carducci himself a believer in the present existence of the Gods of Greece, he could hardly have infused a more intense life into his writing than he has done by the continually suggested presence of the happy gods, sirens, and nymphs of the classic mythology. Our modern poets can use the same mythologic personages in figurative embellishment or in allegoric allusion. In Carducci they are real presences such as Wordsworth sighed for in his sonnet, "The World is too much with us":

> Great God! I'd rather be
> A pagan suckled in a creed outworn, —
> So might I, standing on this pleasant lea,
> Have glimpses that would make me less forlorn;
> Have sight of Proteus rising from the sea;
> Or hear old Triton blow his wreathéd horn!

and as Keats felt when writing in his "Ode on a Grecian Urn" these lines:

> Heard melodies are sweet, but those unheard
> Are sweeter; therefore, ye soft pipes, play on:
> Not to the sensual ear, but, more endear'd,
> Pipe to the spirit ditties of no tone:
>
> . . . .
>
> . . . .
>
> O Attic shape! Fair attitude! with brede
> Of marble men and maidens overwrought,
> With forest branches and the trodden weed;
> Thou silent form! dost tease us out of thought

---

[5] Goethe's Friendship with Schiller. *Fortnightly Review,* Aug., 1891.

As doth eternity.

The same vivid realisation of the presence of the supernatural in nature under truly pagan forms is seen in Carducci's poem "To Aurora" [VII]:

Thou risest and kissest, O Goddess, with rosy breath the clouds,
Kissest the dusky pinnacles of marble temples.

In this poem is contrasted in most realistic manner the Greek sense of the sunlight as a divine presence, imparting only joy to men and leading them to seek their delights under the open sky, with the exhausting nightly dissipations of modern life and the hatred of daylight which recalls men to their labour:

Ours is a wearied race:
Sad is thy face, O Aurora, when thou risest over our towers.
The dim street-lamps go out, and, not even glancing at thee,
A pale-faced troop go home imagining they have been happy.
Angrily at his door is pounding the ill-tempered labourer,
Cursing the dawn that only calls him back to his bondage.

Next to the emotion of the supernatural, we are struck with the intense sympathy with nature both animate and inanimate, which gives so lively a glow to Carducci's description. The sonnet on "The Ox" [IX] I have referred to in the previous essay; here I would call attention to that addressed "To a Horse" [XVII], which, if the former can be called Homeric, can equally claim to be Phidian in the pure outline of the drawing and the Olympic spirit that seems to quiver in the poet's words:

O that for thee might blaze the sands Elean,
For thee great hymns the godlike Pindar sing,
Following thee there upon the waves Alphaean!

Keats proves how deeply he has imbibed the Greek poetic spirit in his sonnet on the "Grasshopper and the Cricket"; for here he expresses the same intense joy of communion with a certain soul in nature which caused Theocritus to never tire of singing, or having his Sicilian goatherds sing, of the bees that fed the imprisoned Comatas all through the springtime, of the Oaks that sung the dirges of the shepherd Daphnis, of the "shegoats feeding on the hill," of "the young lambs pasturing on the upland fields when the spring is on the wane," of "the white calves browsing on the arbutus," of the "cicada to cicada dear," "the prattling locusts," and "lizards that sleep at midday by the dry stone wall."

With the same zest Carducci delights to sing of the "forests awaking with a cool shiver" at the rising of Aurora, of "the garrulous nests that mutter amid the wet leaves" in the early dawn, of the "grey gull far off that screams over the purple sea," "the sorrel colt breaking away with high lifted mane and neighing in the wind," and "the pack of hounds, wakeful, answering from their kennels." What Mr. Lang says of Theocritus may be as truly said of Carducci: "There is nothing in Wordsworth more real, more full of the incommunicable sense of nature.... It is as true to nature as the statue of the native fisherman in the Vatican." [Introduction to *Theocritus*.] Especially are we aware of the almost oppressive feeling of nature's languor and sweet melancholy on reading Carducci's poems on "A Dream in Summer" [XVIII] and "On a Saint Peter's Eve" [XIX]. Here, indeed, the feeling is more modern than ancient, but the mode of expressing it is the same. How like Homer is the picture of

> The sun across the red vapours descending,
> And falling into the sea like a shield of brass
> Which shines wavering over the bloody field of war,
> Then drops and is seen no more.

It seems like the reverse of the figure in the "Iliad," where the armed Diomed is described:

> Forth from his helm and shield a fire-light
> Then flashed, like autumn star that brightest shines
> When newly risen from his ocean bath.

And further, when we read of the swallows that

> Wove and rewove their crooked flight around the gutters,
> While in shadows malarious the brown sparrows were chattering;

and how there comes

> through the humid air
> The song of the reapers, long, distant, mournful and wearied—

a line which can only tell its full tale of tender sadness in the original:

> il canto
> de mietitori, longo, lontano, piangevole, stanco—

how the sun looks down

> like a cyclops heavy with wine—

and we are then as suddenly awakened out of our delicious reverie by the screaming of a peacock and a bat's wing grazing our head, we know that the poetry is real not by its mere accuracy of description, but by the feeling that it awakens as only nature itself could awaken it.

The "Summer Dream" recalls, in the vividness and delicacy of its landscape and tenderness of feeling, perhaps more of Dante than of the ancient poets. There is a vision of the mother walking with the poet's little brother by the river bank,

> the happy mother walking in the sunlight,

which suggests Dante's glimpse of the Countess Matilda in the daisy-sprinkled meadow, described in the twenty-eighth canto of the "Purgatory." The bells of Easter-eve are telling from a high tower that

> on the morrow Christ would rise again.

From the sea far below comes up the odorous breeze, while

> on its waters four white sails rock slowly to and fro in the sun.

The poet's thoughts wander to where, in the solemn shades of Certosa and on the flowering banks of the Arno, lie at rest the beloved ones. But quickly, with the sudden waking from the nap, is dispelled the vision of the poet and with it the modern introspective gloom; these give place to the realism and the day-light contentment of the old time:

> Lauretta's joyous song was ringing through all the chambers
> While Bice,[6] bending over her frame, followed silent the work of the needle.

There is something majestic in the moral portraiture of the poem on "The Mother." [XX] We seem to be looking on a colossal bronze figure, in which are blended pure natural joy and an instinct of the divine holiness of motherhood. The reproach contained in the last verse belongs to the present time of social unrest; it is hard to convey in English the full intent of the subtle phrase:

> la giustizia pia del lavoro—.

Paul Bourget speaks, in his *Sensations d'Italie*, of the simplicity "peculiar to the lofty style of Italian poetry introduced by Dante, under which one feels the glorious origin of the language"; and he quotes, as illustrating this simplicity, Carducci's "divine sonnet" commencing:

> Passa la nave mia, sola, tra il pianto.

[XXI] On this he remarks:

"The quality of the words in which Roman vigour still palpitates, the direct force of the image, the construction, at once flowing and concise, of the sentence, give this poetry the charm of precision which is the distinctive characteristic of the genius of the Romans. It is at once sober and grand." Surely no better example of such writing could anywhere be found than in the poem on "The Mother."

With what awful severity such a style lends itself to the exposure of the corruption and inhumanity of society, like a veritable Juvenal returned to hurl his satire at these modern times, is shown in the poem on "The Carnival." [XXII]

Another phase of Carducci's genuine realism is the subtle art of blending with nature, not his own personality, but that of great souls of the past who have lived amid the scenes described. Of this a fine example is the poem "Sermione" mentioned above. [XVI] The peninsula so named, which juts boldly out into the southern bay of the Lago di Garda, the *Lacus Benacus* of the Romans, is about equidistant from Mantua on the south, the birthplace of Virgil, and from Verona on the east, the birthplace of Catullus. Near by is situated one of the castles of the Scaligers, where Dante may have had his abode when taking refuge with that family on his banishment from Florence in 1316. At the extremity of the promontory are still seen the relics of the villa of Catullus, in which he is supposed to have written many of his poems, especially the one beginning

> Peninsularum, Sirmio, insularumque
> Ocelle.

How endeared was the lake to the tender-hearted poet, and how its cool and

---

[6] Familiar contraction of the name Beatrice.

placid shores brought solace to his bosom, rent with the passions of Rome's giddy life, Carducci tells in the song of the Sirens—

> Come to us, Quintus Valerius!
> Here to our grottos descend still the sunrays, but silvery, and mild as those of Cynthia.
> Here the assiduous tumults that burden thy life but resemble the distant humming of bees.

We feel ourselves to be listening for the poet, and would fain with him enjoy the fresh air, the soothing calm,

> While Hesperus over the waters broadens his rosy face.
> And the waves are lapping the shore.

In the glimpses afforded, in this poem, of Garda lifting her dusky shoulders over the liquid mirror,

> Singing the while a saga of cities ancient and buried,
> And their barbaric kings;

of Catullus,

> Mooring all day long to the wet rocks his pitched canoe
> And watching in the phosphorescent waves the eyes of his Lesbia;

of the

> white swans swimming down through the silvery Mincio;

and,

> from the green pastures where sleeps Bianore, the sound of Virgilius' voice;

and of the

> face stern and grand looking out from the tower of the Scaligers,

centuries of literary history seem to pass before our eyes in living procession.

Most tender of all these tributes of the poet, interweaving the memory of his revered predecessors and masters with the nature loved by them, and by himself for them, is the sonnet addressed to Petrarch [XXIII]:

> If far from turbid thoughts and gloomy mood.

It is as delicate as the odour of jessamine

> in the green blackness of the tangled wood,

and breathes a rich melancholy, as if,

> when day is done,
> A nightingale from bough to bough were singing.

The sonnets addressed to the more recent poets, his fellow-countrymen, seem mainly to have served as vents for Carducci's own indignation at the literary and political degeneracy of the present time. Many of them are from among the poet's earlier productions, and the changes which have occurred since their writing make them seem to belong already to a past period when perhaps more than at present his severe reflections on his country and countrymen were deserved. A foreigner can hardly enter into the bitterness of vituperation which finds utterance in such poems as those "In Santa Croce" [XXVIII], or "The Voice of the Priests" [XXIX], the sonnet addressed to Vittorio Alfieri [XXV],

> O de l'italo agon supremo atleta,

and that to Goldoni, the "Terence of the Adria"; but all of these, which we may call the literary sonnets, have a certain universal value in that they reflect more than individual feeling. Each poet addressed is identified in some way with the nation's weal or woe; and the soul of the patriot, and no mere dilettante admiration, is what pours forth those fervid utterances which, in another tongue and to the ear of strangers, will naturally often seem overwrought.

No less truly does the soul of the father speak in the beautiful verses "On my Daughter's Marriage," and the soul of manly friendship in that little song "At the Table of a Friend," which seems as if it had dropped from the pages of Horace like a purple grape from the cluster all odorous with its bloom.

Over all others in stern and majestic portraiture rise those verses, both of the earlier and later period, in which Carducci treats of Dante and his influence. Nowhere are we more impressed than here with the strange fascination of that man who

> made things good and evil to tell their tale through him the fatal prophet;

against whose Gothic sphere Carducci's Hellenic spirit continually fretted and rebelled. Yet his soul is ever thrilled (see the Sonnet on the Sixth Centenary of Dante [XXXIV]) with awe at the reappearing of that "mighty Form,"

> when shook the Adrian shore and all the land Italia trembled,

which,

> like a morning mist
> Did march along the Apenninian strand,
> Glancing adown the vales on either hand,
> Then vanished like the dawn;

while "in earthly hearts a fear arose, discovering the awful presence of a God," and there,

> where, beyond the gates, the sun is burning,
> The races dead, of war-like men and wise,
> With joy saluted the great soul's returning.

The antagonism between the pagan and the Christian religious instincts comes to light in all that Carducci writes of his revered master. Half in anger he chides the awful singer who

> Comes down from heaven bringing the Hymn Supreme,

while upon his brow shines

a radiance divine
Like his who spake with God in Sinai,—

because he cared not for

His poor country and the endless strife that rent its cities.

With the splendours of the holy kingdom, amid which Dante stood, Carducci contrasts the mortal fields of civil war and the wastes deserted and malignant,

whence comes the sound, dreary and dull, of dying warriors' sighs;

and yet no commentator seems to become so transformed as Carducci into Dante's own being and manner when contemplating and describing him. The poem on Dante, beginning with the words [XXXIII]:

Forte sembianze di novella vita,

recalls, in its statuesque strength and supple beauty, Michael Angelo's "Sleeping Slave." It breathes all through with the spirit of the Italian Renaissance. In the narrative of Dante's secret heart-life and soul-life it seems as if we were turning new leaves of *La Vita Nova* rather than those of a nineteenth-century critic. No voice but Dante's seems to speak in lines like these, describing the first awaking of the passion of love in the youthful poet's heart:

Sighing and pensive, yet with locks aglow
With rosy splendour from another air,
Love made long stay:
And such the gentle things
He talked to thee with bashful lips: so sweetly
He entered all the chambers of thy heart
That no one ever knew to love like thee.

This surely is the "intelletto d'amore" of Dante himself.

Hardly less like Dante is the picture of Beatrice in that half-playful, half-worshipful poem on that mysterious personage [XXXV]:

Like our Lady from heaven
She passes before me,
An angel in seeming, and yet all so ardent
My mind stopped thinking
But to look at her,
And the soul was at rest,—but for sighing!

How sweet and true an echo from Sonnet XXV in *La Vita Nova*:

Tanto gentile e tanto onesta pare!

Here Carducci treats Beatrice under the favourite character of the Idea which is to elevate mankind from its rude savagery. As in Goethe,

Das ewig weibliche zieht uns hinan.

Not a woman, but the Idea,
Am I, which heaven did offer

For man to study when seeking things on high.

Nevertheless, we cannot forget the satirical tone in which, in another poem, he contrasts the ideal love of Dante with the passion of a lower kind that found its home in the Greek nature, and sings rather of Lalage and Lesbia than of this "Angel in seeming."

It is in his poetic power of interpretation that here, as in the poems on nature, Carducci proves himself the true realist. Whatever form he chooses, is for the time filled with its own life, and speaks from that and no other. I have introduced the "Hymn to the Redeemer" [XI], that *Lauda Spirituale*, which the poet describes in the passage from his autobiography quoted in the previous essay as a youthful literary experiment, in which he attempted to clothe the spiritual idea of the Christ with the form of the pagan triumphal ode. The heroic picture of the Redeemer of the world returning from Battle as a Victor and receiving triumphal honour and applause, is novel, and not without a high order of beauty. It seems, indeed, to minds trained to modern religious thought, more pagan than Christian; but one may question whether this aspect of Christ as the Hero is not one which the Church has erroneously overlooked in her tendency to lay stress on the vicarious sacrifice of Christ, rather than on the actual deliverance wrought for man by Him in His warfare against the infernal hosts, setting the race thereby spiritually free from bondage. Do we not see here the same attempt to present the Christian Redemption in ancient heroic form, as the Pisan sculptors made when they copied from pagan sarcophagi the figures of their apostles and saints? It was not the conventional way; but we feel that they might have done worse.

A few poems from Carducci's youthful period, in which he indulges in the meaningless melancholy, the passion and despair, incident to that stage of the poet's growth, I have introduced, as showing that he too had his sentimental side. In these he describes his emotions. They are the sonnets from the *Juvenilia*, beginning respectively with the following lines:

O questi di prima io la vidi. Uscia. [XXXVI]

. . . .

Non son quell'io che già d'amiche cene. [XXXVII]

. . . .

Passa la nave mia, sola, tra il pianto. [XXI]

As such they are beautiful, but they lack that objectivity and realistic power which is felt in those poems where, as in life, the emotion tells itself, and does not need to be described.

In the *Odi Barbare*, for which title I am unable to find a better rendering than "Barbaric Odes," foreign as it may seem to the character of these exquisitely finished verses, I have followed the poet's choice in omitting to capitalize the initial words of the lines. Many of these poems are without rhyme, and, for the sake of greater faithfulness in translating them, I have sometimes discarded both the rhyme and the strict rhythmical form.

F. S.

Washington, D. C., June, 1892.

TRANSLATIONS
POEMS

I

ROMA

Give to the wind thy locks; all glittering
Thy sea-blue eyes, and thy white bosom bared,
Mount to thy chariots, while in speechless roaring
Terror and Force before thee clear the way!

The shadow of thy helmet like the flashing
Of brazen star strikes through the trembling air.
The dust of broken empires, cloud-like rising,
Follows the awful rumbling of thy wheels.

So once, O Rome, beheld the conquered nations

Thy image, object of their ancient dread.[7]
To-day a mitre they would place upon

Thy head, and fold a rosary between
Thy hands. O name! again to terrors old
Awake the tired ages and the world!

Decennali.

---

[7] The allusion is to the figure of "Roma" as seen upon ancient coins.

II

TO SATAN

To thee my verses,
Unbridled and daring,
Shall mount, O Satan,
King of the banquet.

Away with thy sprinkling,
O Priest, and thy droning,
For never shall Satan,
O Priest, stand behind thee.

See how the rust is
Gnawing the mystical
Sword of St. Michael;
And how the faithful

Wind-plucked archangel
Falls into emptiness!
Frozen the thunder in
Hand of Jehovah.

Like to pale meteors, or
Planets exhausted,
Out of the firmament
Rain down the angels.

Here in the matter
Which never sleeps,
King of phenomena,
King of all forms,

Thou, Satan, livest!
Thine is the empire
Felt in the dark eyes'
Tremulous flashing,

Whether their languishing
Glances resist, or,
Glittering and tearful, they
Call and invite.

How shine the clusters

With happy blood,
So that the furious
Joy may not perish!

So that the languishing
Love be restored,
And sorrow be banished
And love be increased!

Thy breath, O Satan,
My verses inspires
When from my bosom
The gods I defy

Of Kings pontifical,
Of Kings inhuman:
Thine is the lightning that
Sets minds to shaking.

For thee Arimane,
Adonis, Astarte;
For thee lived the marbles,
The pictures, the parchments,

When the fair Venus
Anadiomene
Blessed the Ionian
Heavens serene.

For thee were roaring the
Forests of Lebanon,
Of the fair Cyprian
Lover reborn;

For thee rose the chorus,
For thee raved the dances,
For thee the pure shining
Loves of the virgins,

Under the sweet-odoured
Palms of Idume,
Where break in white foam
The Cyprian waves.

What if the barbarous
Nazarene fury,
Fed by the base rites
Of secret feastings,

Lights sacred torches
To burn down the temples,
Scattering abroad
The scrolls hieroglyphic?

In thee find refuge
The humble-roofed plebs,
Who have not forgotten
The gods of their household.

Thence comes the power,
Fervid and loving, that,
Filling the quick-throbbing
Bosom of woman,

Turns to the succour
Of nature enfeebled,
A sorceress pallid,
With endless care laden.

Thou to the trance-holden
Eye of the alchemist,
Thou to the view of the
Bigoted mago,

Showest the lightning-flash
Of the new time
Shining behind the dark
Bars of the cloister.

Seeking to fly from thee
Here in the world-life,
Hides him the gloomy monk
In Theban deserts.

O soul that wanderest
Far from the straight way,
Satan is merciful.
See Héloïsa!

In vain you wear yourself
Thin in rough gown; I
Still murmur the verses
Of Maro and Flaccus

Amid the Davidic
Psalming and wailing;
And—Delphic figures
Close to thy side—

Rosy, amid the dark
Cowls of the friars,
Enters Licorida,
Enters Glicera.

Then other images
Of days more fair
Come to dwell with thee

In thy secret cell.

Lo! from the pages of
Livy, the Tribunes
All ardent, the Consuls,
The crowds tumultuous,

Awake; and the fantastic
Pride of Italian
Drives thee, O Monk,
Up to the Capitol;

And you, whom the flaming
Pyre never melted,
Conjuring voices,
Wiclif and Huss,

Send to the broad breeze
The cry of the watchman:
"The age renews itself;
Full is the time!"

Already tremble
The mitres and crowns.
Forth from the cloister
Moves the rebellion.

Under his stole, see,
Fighting and preaching,
Brother Girolamo
Savonarola.

Off goes the tunic
Of Martin Luther;
Off go the fetters
That bound human thought.

It flashes and lightens,
Girdled with flame.
Matter, exalt thyself!
Satan has won!

A fair and terrible
Monster unchained
Courses the oceans,
Courses the earth;

Flashing and smoking,
Like the volcanoes, he
Climbs over mountains,
Ravages plains,

Skims the abysses;

Then he is lost
In unknown caverns
And ways profound,

Till lo! unconquered,
From shore to shore,
Like to the whirlwind,
He sends forth his cry.

Like to the whirlwind
Spreading its wings...
He passes, O people,
Satan the great!

Hail to thee, Satan!
Hail, the Rebellion!
Hail, of the reason the
Great Vindicator!

Sacred to thee shall rise
Incense and vows!
Thou hast the god
Of the priests disenthroned!

III

HOMER

And from the savage Urals to the plain
A new barbarian folk shall send alarms,
The coast of Agenorean Thebes again
Be waked with sound of chariots and of arms;

And Rome shall fall; and Tiber's current drain
The nameless lands of long-deserted farms:
But thou, like Hercules, shalt still remain,
Untouched by fiery Etna's deadly charms;

And with thy youthful temples laurel-crowned
Shalt rise to the eternal Form's embrace
Whose unveiled smile all earliest was thine;

And till the Alps to gulfing sea give place,
By Latin shore or on Achæan ground,
Like heaven's sun, shalt thou, O Homer, shine!

Levia Gravia.

IV

VIRGIL

As when above the heated fields the moon
Hovers to spread its veil of summer frost,
The brook between its narrow banks half lost
Glitters in pale light, murmuring its low tune;

The nightingale pours forth her secret boon,
Whose strains the lonely traveller accost;
He sees his dear one's golden tresses tossed,
And time forgets in love's entrancing swoon;

And the orphaned mother who has grieved in vain
Upon the tomb looks to the silent skies
And feels their white light on her sorrow shine;

Meanwhile the mountains laugh, and the far-off main,
And through the lofty trees a fresh wind sighs:
Such is thy verse to me, Poet divine!

Levia Gravia.

V

INVOCATION TO THE LYRE

If once I cut thee with a trembling hand
From Latin bough to Phœbus that belongs,
So now, O Lyre, shalt thou rehearse the songs
Of the Tuscan land.

What consolations fierce to bosoms hard
Of bristling warriors thou wast wont to bring,
Or else in peace the soothing verse to sing
Of the Lesbian bard!

Thou taughtest them of Venus and of Love,
And of the immortal son of Semele,
The Lycian's hair, the glowing majesty
Of deep-browed Jove.

Now, when I strike, comes smiling to my side
The spirit of Flaccus, and through choirs divine
Of laurelled nymphs that radiant round me shine,
Calmly I glide.

O dear to Jove and Phœbus! Sway benignant
Which art chief guardian of our cities' peace,
Answer our prayers! and bid the discord cease
Of souls malignant!

Juvenilia.

VI

SUN AND LOVE

Fleecy and white into the western space
Hurry the clouds; the wet sky laughs
Over the market and streets; and the labour of man
Is hailed by the sun, benign, triumphal.

High in the rosy light lifts the cathedral
Its thousand pinnacles white and its saints of gold
Flashing forth its hosannas; while all around
Flutter the wings and the notes of the brown-plumed choir.

So 'tis when love and its sweet smile dispel
The clouds which had so sorely me oppressed;
The sun again arises in my soul
With all life's holiest ideals renewed

And multiplied, the while each thought becomes
A harmony and every sense a song.

Nuove Poesie.

VII

TO AURORA

Thou risest and kissest, O Goddess, with rosy breath, the clouds,
Kissest the dusky pinnacles of marble temples.

The forests feel thee and with a cool shiver awake;
Up soars the falcon flashing in eager joy.

Meanwhile amid the wet leaves mutter the garrulous nests,
And far off the grey gull screams over the purple sea.

First to delight in thee, down in the laborious plain,
Are the streams which glisten amid the rustling poplars.

Daringly the sorrel colt breaks away from his feeding,
Runs to the brooks with high-lifted mane, neighing in the wind.

Wakeful answers from the huts the great pack of the hounds,
And the whole valley is filled with the sound of their noisy barking.

But the man whom thou awakest to life-consuming labour,
He, O ancient Youth, O Youth eternal,

Still thoughtful admires thee, even as on the mountain
The Aryan Fathers adored thee, standing amid their white oxen.

Again upon the wing of the fresh morning flies forth
The hymn which to thee they sang over their heaped-up spears.

"Shepherdess thou of heaven! from the stalls of thy jealous sister
Thou loosest the rosy kine and leadest them back to the skies:

Thou leadest the rosy kine, and the white herds, and the horses
With the blond flowing manes dear to the brothers Asvini."

Like a youthful bride who goes from her bath to her spouse,
Reflecting in her eyes the love of him her lover,

So dost thou smiling let fall the light garments that veil thee,
And serene to the heavens thy virgin figure reveal.

Flushed thy cheeks, with white breast panting, thou runnest
To the sovereign of worlds, to the fair flaming Suria.

And he joins and, in a bow, stretches around his mighty neck
Thy rosy arms: but at his terrible glances thou fleest.

'Tis then the Asvinian Twins, the cavaliers of heaven,
Welcome thee rosily trembling in thy chariot of gold,

And thither thou turnest where, measured the road of glory,
Wearied, the god awaits thee in the dull gloaming of eve.

"Gracious thy flight be above us!" so invoked thee the fathers,
"Gracious the going of thy radiant car over our houses.

"Come from the coasts of the East with thy good fortune,
Come, with thy flowering oats and thy foaming milk.

"And in the midst of the calves, dancing, with yellow locks,
An offspring vast shall adore thee, O Shepherdess of heaven!"

So sang the Aryans. But better pleased thee Hymettus,
Fresh with the twenty brooks whose banks smelt to heaven of thyme;

Better pleased thee on Hymettus the nimble-limbed, mortal huntsman,
Who with the buskined foot pressed the first dews of the morn.

The heavens bent down. A sweet blush tinged the forest and the hills,
When thou, O Goddess, didst descend.

But thou descendedst not; rather did Cephalus, drawn by thy kiss,
Mount, all alert, through the air, fair as a beautiful god,—

Mount on the amorous winds and amid the sweet odours,
While all around were the nuptials of flowers and the marriage of
streams.

Wet lies upon his neck the heavy tress of gold and the golden quiver
Reaches above his white shoulder, held by the belt of vermilion.

O fragrant kisses of a goddess among the dews!
O ambrosia of love in the world's youth-time!

Dost thou also love, O goddess? But ours is a wearied race;
Sad is thy face, O Aurora, when thou risest over our towers.

The dim street-lamps go out; and without even glancing at thee,
A pale-faced troop go home imagining they have been happy.

Angrily at his door is pounding the ill-tempered labourer,
Cursing the dawn that only calls him back to his bondage.

Only the lover, perhaps, fresh from the dreams of the loved one,
His blood still warm from her kisses, salutes thee with joy,

Beholds with delight thy face, and feels thy cool breathing upon him:
Then cries, "O bear me, Aurora, upon thy swift courser of flame,—

"Bear me up into the fields of the stars, that there, looking down,
I may behold the earth beneath thy rosy light smiling,—

"Behold my fair one in the face of the rising day,
Let fall her black tresses down over her blushing bosom."

Odi Barbare.

VIII

RUIT HORA

O green and silent solitudes far from the rumours of men!
Hither come to meet us true friends divine, O Lidia,
Wine and love.

O tell me why the sea far under the flaming Hesperus
Sends such mysterious moanings; and what songs are these, O Lidia,
The pines are chanting?

See with what longing the hills stretch their arms to the setting sun!
The shadow lengthens and holds them; they seem to be asking
A last kiss, O Lidia!

ODI BARBARE.

IX

THE OX

T'amo, pio bove

I love thee, pious ox; a gentle feeling
Of vigour and of peace thou giv'st my heart.
How solemn, like a monument, thou art!
Over wide fertile fields thy calm gaze stealing,
Unto the yoke with grave contentment kneeling,
To man's quick work thou dost thy strength impart.
He shouts and goads, and answering thy smart,
Thou turn'st on him thy patient eyes appealing.

From thy broad nostrils, black and wet, arise
Thy breath's soft fumes; and on the still air swells,
Like happy hymn, thy lowing's mellow strain.
In the grave sweetness of thy tranquil eyes
Of emerald, broad and still reflected dwells
All the divine green silence of the plain.

X

TO PHŒBUS APOLLO

The sovereign driver
Of the ethereal chariot
Whips the fiery wing-footed steeds—
A Titan most beautiful.

. . . .

From the Thessalian valley,
From the Ægean shores,
The vision divine of the prophets
Hellenic saw thee arise,

The youthful god most fair;
Rising through the deserted skies,
Thy feet had wings of fire,
Thy chariot was a flame,

And around thee danced
In the sphere serene
The twenty-four virgins,
In colours tawny and bright.

Didst thou not live? Did the
Mæonian verse never reach thee?
And did Proclus in vain call thee
The Love of the universe?

The inexorable truth
With its cold shadow covered
Thee, the phantom of ages past,
Hellas' god and mine.

Now, where is the chariot and the golden,
Radiant brow of youth?
An unsightly mouldering heap
Gloomily flashing remains.

Alas, from the Ausonian lands
All the gods are flown!
In a vast solitude
Thou remainest, my Muse.

In vain, O Ionian virgin,
Thy songs and thy calling on Homer;
Truth, the sallow-faced, rises
From her deserts and threatens.

Farewell, O Titan Apollo,
Who governed the rolling year;
Alone is left to lead me
Love, the last delusion.

Let us go: in the acts and the smiles
Of my Delia still do the Graces
Reveal themselves, as of old
Cephisus beheld them.

Perish the sober age
That quenches the life in me,
That freezes in souls Phœbean
The Hellenic song!

JUVENILIA.

XI

HYMN TO THE REDEEMER

(For the Feast of Corpus Domini)

Open, O human race,
Open wide the gates!
Behold there comes to you a mighty One,
Who brings you glory and has conquered death.

Before Him let no sound of fear arise,
No sad complaints from dolorous companies.
All nature makes a feast as if to adorn
Herself, in presence of the coming Spouse.
Bring then, O Children, scatter in the way
The immortal laurel and the blushing rose
With the pure whiteness of the jessamine.

Behold He comes, the mighty King encrowned
With victory's trophies hither to your midst.
Before His face fly Death and Sin away,
While Peace and Health move at His either side.
Behold the Lord who of rebellious man
Suffered Himself the doom
And payed our ransom with His own heart's blood.

He made Himself the fellow of our grief,
He bore our burden and endured our shame.
Black over Him did fall the shadow of death.
Nor turned the Father to His cry the face—
That day when, seeing again the sacred Mount,
Came from their tombs
The prophets and the saints of Israel!

Behold the Isaac of the ancient time,
Who bends beneath the sword his gentle neck
And looks upon his slayer with a smile,
Kneeling to him in all humility.
No pity for the blooming flower of youth;
None for that bitter end,
Nor for the robbed embraces of the mother.

And now, His death forever witnessing,
He brings with Him Divine Humanity,
Irradiating all the earth with joy
As when the sun dispels the gloomy cloud;
And all the abodes of woe and that dark land
Where dwelt the shadow of death
He comforts with His presence all divine.

To Him upon His throne of victory
Be lifted up the gaze of every art,
Whom glory like a cloud doth gird around
And love angelical encompasseth.
Fly thither from the world where grief still sighs,
Where death still bides and reigns,
Fly, O my song, to Him who thee deserves,

And there relate the sorrows of His people
Who, from the good astray, still seek the good,
Like hart that panteth for the cooling stream,
Or bird imprisoned for its native air:
He from the sphere divine wherein He dwells
May send a ray benign
To souls perplexed and lost in their life's way.

Lift, O human race,
Lift up your minds
And chastened hearts to this most clement King,
Who welcomes those who turn to Him in faith!

JUVENILIA.

XII

OUTSIDE THE CERTOSA

The dead are saying: "Blessed are ye who walk along the hillsides
Flooded with the warm rays of the golden sun.

"Cool murmur the waters through flowery slopes descending.
Singing are the birds to the verdure, singing the leaves to the wind.

"For you are smiling the flowers ever new on the earth;
For you smile the stars, the flowers eternal of heaven."

The dead are saying: "Gather the flowers, for they too pass away;
Adore the stars, for they pass never away.

"Rotted away are the garlands that lay around our damp skulls.
Roses place ye around the tresses golden and black.

"Down here it is cold. We are alone. Oh, love ye the sun!
Shine, constant star of Love, on the life which passes away!"

ODI BARBARE.

XIII

DANTE

O Dante, why is it that I adoring
Still lift my songs and vows to thy stern face,
And sunset to the morning grey gives place
To find me still thy restless verse exploring?

Lucia prays not for my poor soul's resting;
For me Matilda tends no sacred fount;
For me in vain the sacred lovers mount,
O'er star and star to the eternal soaring.

I hate the Holy Empire, and the crown
And sword alike relentless would have riven
From thy good Frederic on Olona's plains.

Empire and Church to ruin have gone down,
And yet for them thy songs did scale high heaven.
Great Jove is dead. Only the song remains.

Levia Gravia.

XIV

IN A GOTHIC CHURCH

They rise aloft, marching in awful file,
The polished shafts immense of marble grey,
And in the sacred darkness seem to be
An army of giants

Who wage a war with the invisible;
The silent arches soar and spring apart
In distant flight, then re-embrace again
And droop on high.

So in the discord of unhappy men,
From out their barbarous tumult there go up
To God the sighs of solitary souls
In Him united.

Of you I ask no God, ye marble shafts,
Ye airy vaults! I tremble—but I watch
To hear a dainty well-known footstep waken
The solemn echoes.

'Tis Lidia, and she turns, and, slowly turning,
Her tresses full of light reveal themselves,
And love is shining from a pale shy face
Behind the veil.

XV

INNANZI, INNANZI!

On, on! through dusky shadows up the hill
Stretches the shining level of the snow,
Which yields and creaks each laboured step I go,
My breath preceding in a vapour chill.

Now silent all. There where the clouds stand still
The moon leaps forth into the blank, to throw
An awful shadow, a gaunt pine below,
Of branches crossed and bent in manner ill.

They seem like the uneasy thought of death.
O Winter vast, embrace me and quick stay
In icy hold my heart's tempestuous waves!
For yet that thought, shipwrecked, again draws breath,
And cries to heaven: O Night, O Winter, say,
What are the dead doing down there in their graves?

XVI

SERMIONE

"Peninsularum, Sirmio, insularumque
Ocelle." —CATULLUS.

See how green Sermio laughs in the lake's lucid waters,
she the peninsula's flower!

The Sun pours down his caresses, while, all around, the Benaco
shines like a great silver cup

along whose rim is entwined a wreath of peaceful olive
mixed with the laurel eternal;

and so the radiant goblet Italia the Mother holds forth
with lofty arms to the gods;

and they from the skies have let thee fall in, O Sermio,
thee, the peninsular jewel!

Above, the paternal mountain boldly stands guard o'er thy beauty,
watching with gloomy eyebrow.

Beneath lies the land like a Titan slain in some desperate battle,
prostrate, but threatening revenge.

But along the curved shores of the bay at the left of the mountain
stretch out the fair white arms

like unto those of a child who, happy on entering the dance,
throws to the breeze her hair,

laughs, and with generous hand deals out her flowers right and left,
and crowns the chief youth with her garland.

Garda there, far below, lifts up her dusky shoulders
over the liquid mirror,

singing the while a saga of cities ancient and buried,
and their barbaric kings.

But here, O Lalage, whence, through the holy joys of the azure,
thou sendest thy soul-glance;

here Valerius Catullus moored to the wet rocks, of old,
his frail pitched canoe,

sat through the long days and watched in the waves, phosphorescent
and tremulous,
the eyes of his Lesbia;

yea, and saw in those waves the changing moods of his Lesbia,
saw her perfidious smile,

the while she beguiled with her charms, through darksome haunts of the
town,
the princely nephews of Romulus.

To him from the humid depths sang forth the nymph of the lake,
"Come to us, Quintus Valerius!

"Here to our grottoes descend still the sun rays, but silvery
and mild as those of Cynthia.

"Here the assiduous tumults that burden thy life but resemble
the distant humming of bees,

"and, in the silence cool, thy cares, all frenzied and fearful,
gently fade into oblivion.

"Here the fresh air, here the sleep, the soothing music and chorus
of the cerulean virgins,

"while Hesperus over the waters broadens his rosy face,
and the waves are lapping the shore."

Alas for sad Love! how the Muses he hates; how the poet he shatters
with lust, or with jealousy kills!

But who from thine eyes and the wars they are plotting afar,
O Lalage, who shall protect?

Pluck for the Muses three boughs of sacred laurel and myrtle,
wave them in sunlight eternal!

Seest thou not from Peschiera how the flocks of white swans are swim-
ming
down through the silvery Mincio?

Dost thou not hear from the green pastures where sleeps Bianore
the sound of Virgilius' voice?

O Lalage, turn and adore! From yonder tower of the Scaligers
looks out a face stern and grand.

"Suso in Italia bella," smiling he murmurs, and looks
at the water, the earth, and the sky.

Odi Barbare.

XVII

TO A HORSE

Hail to thee, valiant steed! To thee the palm,
To thee its wild applause the ring is raising.
Who slanders thee sings an ignoble psalm,
In vain his own poor wit and judgment praising.

Thy body, fair as with no shining balm,
But with the spirit's inward ardour blazing,
Speeds to the prize. Then in what beauty calm
Dost thou stand still, upon thy rivals gazing!

Thou wouldst have been among the conquering
To gain for brave Automedon the pæan
That once from Grecian lips did joyous ring!

O, that for thee might blaze the sands Elean,
For thee great hymns the godlike Pindar sing,
Following thee there upon the waves Alphaean!

Juvenilia.

XVIII

A DREAM IN SUMMER

In the midst of thy song, O Homer, with battles ever resounding,
the midsummer heat overcame me; my head fell asleep
there on Scamander's bank; but my heart fled at once,
as soon as set free, back again to the shore of Tyrrhenia.

I dreamed—dreamed pleasant things of the new years coming to me,
of books no more! My chamber, stifled with the heat of the July sun,
and noisy with the endless rolling of carriages in the streets,
opened wide. I dreamed myself among my hills,—
the dear forest hills which an April-time youth was reflowering.
A stream gushed down the hillside, widening into a brook
with murmuring cool, and along the brook wandered my mother,
still in the flower of her youth, and leading a child by the hand.
On his bare white shoulder lay shining his golden curls.
He walked with a childish step, but stately, too,
proud of the mother's love, and thrilled to the heart
with the great gladness of that Festival
which everywhere sweet Nature was intoning.
For high up in yon tower the bells were telling
that on the morrow Christ would rise again!
And over the hills and vales, through air and boughs and streams,
flowed everywhere the great Hymn of the Spring.
The apple-trees and the peach-trees were blossoming white and red,
underneath laughed the meadow with yellow flowers and blue;
the red trefoil was clambering up to cover the sloping fields,
and beyond the hills lay veiled in the glow of the golden broom.
From the sea below came up an odorous breeze;
on its waters four white sails rocked slowly to and fro in the sun,
whose dazzling rays were quivering over sea and land and sky.
I watched the happy mother walking in the sunlight;
I watched the mother: thoughtful I watched my brother,
him who now lies at rest on the flowering banks of the Arno,
while she is sleeping alone in the solemn shade of Certosa.
Thoughtful I gazed, and wondered if still they live,
and, mindful of my grief, come back from where
their happy years glide on 'mid forms well known.

So passed the vision blessed; quick with my nap it went—

. . . .

Lauretta's joyous song was ringing through all the chambers,
and Bice, bending over her frame, followed silent the work of the needle.

Odi Barbare.

XIX

ON A SAINT PETER'S EVE

I remember the sun across the red vapours descending,
and falling into the sea like a great shield of brass,
which shines wavering over the bloody field of war,
then drops and is seen no more.
Little Castiglioncello, high amid heaps of oaks,
blushing in her glazed windows, returned a coquettish smile.
I, meanwhile, languid and sad [with fever still lingering in me,
and my nerves all heavy and lifeless as if they were weighted with lead],
looked from my window. Swiftly the swallows
wove and rewove their crooked flight around the eaves,
while in shadows malarious the brown sparrows were chattering.
Beyond the wood were the varied hills and the plain
partly razed by the scythe, partly still yellow and waving.
Away through the grey furrows rose the smoke of the smouldering
stubble,
and whether or no did there come through the humid air
the song of the reapers, long, distant, mournful, and wearied?
Everywhere brooded a heaviness, in the air, in the woods, on the shore.
I gazed at the falling sun—"Proud light of the world,
Like a Cyclops heavy with wine thou lookest down on our life"—
Then screamed the peacocks, mocking me from among the pomegran-
ates,
and a vagrant bat as it passed me grazed my head.

Odi Barbare.

XX

THE MOTHER

[A GROUP BY ADRIAN CECIONI]

Surely admired her the rosy day-dawn when,
summoning the farmers to the still grey fields,
it saw her barefooted, with quick step passing
among the dewy odours of the hay.

Heard her at midday the elm-trees white with dust,
as, with broad shoulders bent o'er the yellow winrows,
she challenges in cheery song the grasshoppers
whose hoarse chirping rings from the hot hillsides.

And when from her toil she lifted her turgid bosom,
her sunbrowned face with glossy curls surrounded,
how, then, thy vesper fires, O Tuscany,
did richly tinge with colour her bold figure!

'T is then the strong mother plays at ball with her infant,
the lusty child whom her naked breasts have just sated:
tosses him on high and prattles sweetly with him,
while he, with eye fixed on the shining eyes of his mother,

his little body trembling all over with fear, holds out
his tiny fingers imploring; then loud laughs the mother,
and into the one great embrace of love
lets him fall clasped close to her bosom.

Around her smiles the scene of homely labor;
tremulous nod the oats on the green hillsides;
one hears the distant mooing of the ox,
and on the barn roof the gay plumed cock is crowing.

. . . .

Nature has her brave ones who for her despise
the masks of glory dear to the vulgar throng.
'T is thus, O Adrian, with holy visions
thou comfortest the souls of fellow-men.

'T is thus, O artist, with thy blow severe
thou putt'st in stone the ages' ancient hope,

the lofty hope that cries, "O when shall labor
be happy? and faithful love secure from harm?"

When shall a mighty nation of freemen
say in the face of the sun: "Shine no more
on the idle ease and the selfish wars of tyrants;
but on the pious justice of labour" —?

ODI BARBARE.

XXI

"PASSA LA NAVE MIA, SOLA, TRA IL PIANTO"

My lonely bark beneath the seagull's screaming
Pursues her way across the stormy sea;
Around her mingle, in tumultuous glee,
The roar of waters and the lightning's gleaming.

And memory, down whose face the tears are streaming,
Looks for the shore it can no longer see;
While hope, that struggled long and wearily
With broken oar, at last gives up its dreaming.

Still at the helm erect my spirit stands,
Gazing at sea and sky, and bravely crying
Amid the howling winds and groaning strands:
Sail on, sail on, O crew, all fates defying,
Till at the gate of dark oblivion's lands
We see afar the white shores of the dying.

JUVENILIA.

XXII

CARNIVAL

VOICE FROM THE PALACE

Couldst thou, O north wind, coming
From the deep bosom of the moaning valley,
Or, wandering in the aisles of songful pines,
Or through a lonely cloister's corridors,
Chant to me in a thousand sounds—
The piping of reeds, the roaring of wild beasts,
And cries of human woe!
That would be my delight, the while I know
On yon cold height there lies the winter's snow.

A shower of white darkness
Fills all the sleepy air; the snowy plain
Fades into the horizon far away.
Meanwhile, the sun's great disk grows faintly red
As wearily it sinks behind the clouds,
Staring as 'twere a lidless human eye.
No breeze, no breath among the hills is stirred,
Nor traveller's voice, nor song of children heard,

But the loud crash of branches
Too heavily bent by burden of the snow,
And sharp explosions of the cracking ice,
Arcadia sing and Zephyrus invite
To your sweet company in meadows fair.
Now nature's mute and haughty horror doth
Add zest to pleasure! Come, Eurilla, make
The drowsy coals a livelier sparkle take!

On me let them be casting
A light serenely flashing, such as spring
Doth carry with her wheresoever she goeth.
The mouthing actor
No more the boxes heed, when 'mid the sight
Of all that crowded brilliancy and beauty,
And perfumed tresses, and enwreathéd flowers,
There comes the scent of April's fruitful showers.

VOICE FROM THE HOVEL

O if, with living blood
From my heart streaming, I could thee restore,
Poor, frozen body of my little son!
But my heart dies within me,
And feeble is the hold of my embraces,
And man is deaf and God above too high.
Lay, my poor little one, thy tear-wet cheek
Close to thy mother's whilst I with thee speak.

Not so thy brother lay;
Hardly he drew amid the stifling snow
His failing breath, as on his way he crept.
After the toilsome day,
Beneath a heavy load, his little steps
Failed to keep even pace with th' hurrying men,
While the rough path and the night's stormy frown
Conspired with man to drag his courage down.

The gusts of whirling snow
Beat through his ragged clothes, his wearied limbs.
He falls, and, bleeding, tries to lift himself,
But 'tis in vain; and hunger
Now drains his little strength, and at the end
Of the dolorous way he gives the struggle over;
Then pious Death comes down and looks upon
The bruiséd form; and from its grave of snow
Home to the mother's roof they bring it so.

Alas! with better reason
The eagle flies for refuge from the blast
Unto her eyrie on the jagged cliff,
And the aged beast to his cave.
A kennel warm protects the mastiff's sleep,
Full fed, within the palace there, near by
To where, O child, born of love's mightier breath,
An icy hand leads thee away to death.

VOICE FROM THE BANQUET

Pour! and keep on pouring,
The vintage which the ancient Rhine doth yield,
Crowned with her hundred castles!
Let it foam and bubble
Forth to our sight, and then deep in the breast
Tell what rare treasure hath the sun matured
Within the hills which well may England crave,
And France, land of good wines and heroes brave!

Then let the maddening dance
Whirl thee away! O what a waving sea
Of tresses blond and dark all proudly blending!
O the hot breath that mingles
Itself with thine! O roses quickly faded!
O eyes that know to exchange the hasty flash
The while, of a thousand mingled notes the strain
Pours forth the sigh of pleasure acute to pain!

O sweet deflowering
Of burning cheeks, and pressure of hand in hand,
The hurried beating of the breast near breast,
The cunning strategy,
Now in the ear to lodge the precious secret,
The little parleys carried on by smiles,
The sweet imagining of joys that hide
'Neath her shy glance one presses at his side.

See how from these our feasts
The common people get the benefit,
And civil charity finds large increase!
Thanks to the heavenly power
That ill and good allots, a judgment stern
Has easement in a graceful piety;
And we the happy progeny of mirth,
Shed like the sun a radiance o'er the earth!

VOICE FROM THE GARRET.

The bread gave out, the work
Fell off on which did hang our life,
And trembling sat before the fireless hearth
My mother, and watched me.
Pale was the face and mute with some great fear
The while she watched: until, as if pursued
By that mute stare, after the long, long day
I could endure no more, and stole away.

Down through the winter's mist
Poured the high moon a livid radiance
Above the muddy alley, then disappeared
Behind the clouds. So did
The light of youth but shine to disappear
Upon the sorrow-mingled pathway of my life.
A hand touched me. I felt a foul glance fall
Upon me, and words that did my heart appal.

Appal! but more appalling
The hunger, O ye proud ones, that did drive me,

And the old mother's mute and maddening stare!
And so it came that I took bread to her!
But all desire for me her fast had stilled.
Hardly on me she raised her heavy eyes,
While I on my poor mother's breast would claim
A place where I might hide my face and shame.

Adieu, O tearful visions
Of a once holy love and you, the fond
Companions of a maiden most unhappy!
For you may shine the whiteness
Of that pure veil the mother, weeping, binds!
For you the thought that to the cradle turns;—
I, to my sin abandoned, keep me near
The track of darkness and, so, disappear.

VOICE FROM BENEATH.

Be still, thou maiden sad,
Be still, O grieving mother, and thou, child,
Found starving, when shut down the night's great gloom!
Behold! what festive lights
Gleam in the palace windows, where unite
The ruling orders of our favoured land,
And magistrates and soldiers of renown,
And doctors, mix with merchants of the town.

The bloom of thy best years
Thou spoilest, girl, while thou dost pine in vain
For that sweet love and life that all desire.
Laugh rather, and be gay,
In dazzling robes of silk and gold held up
By hand fair as a countess's, while you haste
To join the dance! Then weep and wait—what for?
The garb of shame that's waiting at thy door!

As if the tears had frozen
Between the eyelids of the dying boy
Whom thou couldst not revive, O wretched mother,
And turned to precious gems,
So shines the fillet in the dame's black hair,
With whom the economist, gallant and suave,
Holds speech! His lips a smile do wear,
As if a kiss each honied word did bear.

Seize and enjoy your triumph,
O Masks! so happy and so powerful.
And when the coming dawn drives folk to work,
Go out and show yourselves,

Belching your ill-digested orgies forth;
Flaunting your pomp before their humble fast;
Nor dream the day when, at your gilded gate,
Grim Hunger and his brother Death shall wait.

Levia Gravia.

XXIII

F. PETRARCA

If far from turbid thoughts and gloomy mood
Some smiling day should see my wish fulfilled
Where breathe the vales with gentle brooks enrilled
The soft air of my Tuscan neighbourhood,
There, where is heard no more the garrulous brood
Of thoughtless minds, in deep oblivion stilled,
Would I to thee my heart's pure altar build
In the green blackness of the tangled wood.

There with the dying splendours of the sun
Thy song should glow amid the flowers springing
On breezy banks where whispering streams do run;
As if, still sweeter sounds and odours flinging
Upward to heaven when the day is done,
A nightingale from bough to bough were singing.

Levia Gravia.

XXIV

CARLO GOLDONI

O Terence of the Adria, to whose pen
Italia's land did give such vengeful power
That, as from rebel soil a noble flower,
So rose alive the Latin soul again.

See! where should rule a race of noble men,
Sharing in righteous deal their bounteous dower,
There art, beshadowed with base passion's glower,
Goes reeling to the jeering harlot's den!

Laugh! and drive out these Goths, and of their shame
Tear down the altars, and to the muse impart
The laurel crown the ancients loved to view.
But no! To-day thou hast no dower but blame;
And the base crowd proclaims in vileness new
How low has fallen our Italian art!

JUVENILIA.

XXV

VITTORIO ALFIERI

"O de l'italo agon supremo atleta"

O supreme wrestler on Italia's plains!
See how a race grown feeble and despairing,
Even from thee the sacred laurel tearing,
The rising of thy holy wrath restrains!

To what high prize thou hold'st the guiding reins,
Whither aloft the stars with thee are faring,
The while the age, to its vile feasts repairing,
Each day tastes viands new and still complains.

"Ungrateful world, O son; and made still worse
By listless souls who on their way proceed
With neither word of chiding nor of praising.
And where to evil thought is linked the curse
Of instincts vile, what heart or mind can read
Those distant heights on which my soul is gazing!"

Juvenilia.

XXVI

VINCENZO MONTI

When burst thy rapid songs from out a brain
A god had struck, his ready kindred knowing,
In mighty flood like that which from the plain
Of Eridanus to the sea is going,

Then rose the immortal siren whose domain
Holds Virgil's ashes, and her breath bestowing
As from an ancient urn disturbed again,
Sweet harmonies as of lyres and reeds were flowing.

Along the circling shores its measures flinging
Came as of bees hid in Ravenna's gloom
The Tuscan verse of Dante softly ringing;
The Po sent back its trumpet note of doom.
Thou ceased. No more was heard the holy singing,
Virgil was still, and Allighieri's tomb.

Juvenilia.

XXVII

GIOVAN BATTISTA NICCOLINI

The time will come when the ancient mother, raising
Her eyes upon the examples of the past,
Shall see our land its lot with virtue cast,
And virtuous souls virtue as friend appraising.

But now, from where the Alpine herds are grazing
To far Sicilian shore, in slumber fast
Like jealous nurse she lulls them to the last,
Lest they should wake and on those forms be gazing.

What worth to thee our feeble note of praise,
Only the people's lullaby to mar?
To thee but shame, to us but harm befalling!
O happy those who 'mid the din of war,
On thee, a prophet worthy of better days,
With Dante and Vittorio shall be calling!

Juvenilia.

XXVIII

IN SANTA CROCE

O great Ones born in that our Nation's hour
To which the world did long look back admiring
As to a springtime when the heavens' inspiring
Poured equal gifts of anger, love, and power,

For slavery has Italia sold her dower,
And feasts with those against her weal conspiring;
At your high shrines in vain were my requiring
Of what may soothe the griefs that on me lower.

The present race such ancestry belying
Seeks but the ease of death, as in its tomb.
Here lives, and only here, the ancient Nation!
And here I stay shivering amid the gloom,
Breathing upon the world my imprecation,
Doomed to live ever by my scorn undying.

Juvenilia.

XXIX

VOICE OF THE PRIESTS

O school of vileness, treachery and lying,
"Asylum of the oppressed," in evil days
Sounding to heaven the cruel oppressor's praise,
While God and King and Fatherland denying!

O wicked was your heartless justifying,
Your benediction on the torturer's blaze,
Your curses on the doomed who dared to raise
A voice against thy tyranny outcrying.

Ready the Empire's brutal force to crave,
Thou smil'st upon its prize unjustly won;
God's prophet is become a lying knave.
O saddest day the sun e'er shone upon
When cowers the Cross, the standard of the slave,
And Christ is made the tyrant's champion!

Juvenilia.

XXX

VOICE OF GOD

Hark! In the temple the voice of God is sounding.
"O people of one speech and one endeavour
Yours is the land with my best gifts abounding
Whereon the smile of heaven is resting ever!

"Away the armed hosts your gates surrounding!
The barbarous hordes that come your speech to sever,
To raze the fortunes of your fathers' founding,
And call you slaves! That will I pardon never!

"Rather within your tombs the flame be stirred
As from an awful flash in heaven burning,
Such as gave forth the Maccabean's word."
Hail Voice divine! be ours the quick discerning
Of what thy message means: in thee be heard
Savonarola's spirit to us returning!

JUVENILIA.

XXXI

ON MY DAUGHTER'S MARRIAGE

O born when over my poor roof did pass
hope like a homeless, wandering nightingale,
and I, disdainful of the present world,
knocked fretful at the portals of the morrow;

now that I stand as at my journey's end,
and see around my threshold flocking come,
in turn, the jackdaws' noisy company,
screaming their flattering plaudits at my door;

't is thou, my dove, dost steal thyself away,
willing a new nest for thyself to weave
beyond the Apennines, where thou may'st feel
the native sweet air of the Tuscan hills.

Go then with love; go then with joy: O go
with all thy pure white faith! The eye
grows dim in gazing at the flying sail.
Meanwhile my Camena is still and thinks, —

thinks of the days when thou, my little one,
went gathering flowers beneath the acacia-trees,
and she who led thee gently by the hand
was reading visions fanciful in heaven, —

thinks of the days when over thy soft tresses
were breathed in the wild ecstasy of freedom
my strophes aimed against the oligarchs
and the base cringing slaves of Italy.

Meanwhile didst thou grow on, a thoughtful virgin,
and she our country with intrepid step
began to climb the lofty heights of art,
to plant thereon the flag of liberty.

Looks back and thinks! — Across the path of years
With thee shall it be sweet one day to dream
the old sweet dreams again, while gazing fondly
upon the smiling faces of thy sons?

Or shall it be my better destiny

to fight on till the sacred summons comes?
Then, O my daughter, let no Beatrice
my soul upon its heavenward flight attend, —

then, on that way where Homer of the Greeks
and Christian Dante long ago did pass,
there be thy gentle look my only guide,
thy voice familiar all my company.

XXXII

AT THE TABLE OF A FRIEND

Not since when on me a child
Heaven's gracious radiance smiled
Hast thou, O Sun, such splendour poured
As on my friend's Livornian board.

Never, O God of Feasts, was sent
A solace so benevolent
As wisely glowed within the wines
We drank beneath the Apennines.

O Sun, O Bromius, grant that whole
In loving heart and virtuous soul
We to the quiet shades descend
(Where Horace is)—I and my friend.

Thy fortune smile upon the young
Like flowers around our banquet flung;
Peace to the mothers give, and fame
To valiant youth and love's sweet flame!

ODI BARBARE.

XXXIII

DANTE

Strong forms were those of the New Life, that stood
Around thy cradle,
O Master of the song that looks above!

A brave young giantess,
Unknown before to Greek or Latin shores,
Daring in love and hate, and fair withal,
Came Tuscan Libertade, and the child
Already with bounteous breast did comfort thee.

And all a-glowing with her spheral rays,
Mild and austere in one,
Came Faith: and she, across a shore
Obscure with crowds of visions and of shades,
Opened for thee the Gate of the Infinite.

Sighing and pensive, yet with locks aglow
With rosy splendour from another air,
Love made long stay.
And such the gentle things
He talked to thee with bashful lips, so sweetly
He entered all the chambers of thy heart,
That no one ever knew to love like thee.

But soon away from lonely meditating,
O youthful recluse,
Wild clamour and fierce tumult tore thee, and
The fury of brothers seeking brothers' blood.
Thou heard'st the hissing flames of civil war
On neighbour's walls; thou heardest women shriek
To heaven that altars and the marriage bed,
The dear hearth-stone and the infant's cradle, —
All that made fair the marital abode,
Were swept away in one great gulf of flame.
Their men had rushed from their embrace to arms;
The youth breathed only anger and destruction.
Thou sawest the raging of swords
Seeking the breast-plunge;

Thou heardest the dying warrior
Blaspheme and curse:
Before thee, streaming with gore,
Gold locks and grey;
And the Furies offering
To Liberty the execrated host
Of human victims;
And Death, the cruel arbiter of fates,
Crumbling the mighty towers and opening
The long-barred gates.
Amid wild scenes
So grew thy Italian soul,
And prayed that the long civil hate might end.

Meanwhile he saw
Of love such pure revealings and so strange,
The which depicted in the shade
Of a young myrtle-tree,
Each one who saw must bow the head in reverence.

But o'er this gentle dream
There came the voice of weeping,
Bitterly sounding from the maternal source.
Alas! broken by the whirlwind,
Lies the fair myrtle,
And with wide-spread wings
The dove of sweet affection is flown forth
To seek a purer aura for its flight.

He, driven here and there
In the thick darkness of the turbulent age,
Sought refuge with the famous shades of old;
So learned to hate himself and present things.
And in the twilight came he forth a giant,
Seeming a shade himself—an angry shade
Who through the desert went from tomb to tomb,
Now questioning and now embracing them:
Until before him rose across the ruin
And dust of these barbaric ages gone,
Like a cloudy pillar, the ancient Latin valour.
Then all that such a ruin tells did burst
Upon the silent air in one great cry.
In the exalted vision
Arose the poet divine; and now, disdaining
His stricken land and time that only wasted
In petty aimless strife the ancient strength,
He, in the seeing of his heart's desire,
Saluted thee, O modern Italy,—

One, in thy valiant arms, thy laws, thy speech.

And then, to truly tell
What such a vision meant, he sought to know
The life that rolls through all the sea of being.
From beneath the dust of buried centuries
He made things good and ill to tell their tale
Through him the fatal prophet: till his voice
Resounded through the world, and made the ages
Turn and behold themselves. Judge and lord,
He placed them where they could themselves behold,
Admired and wept, disdained and laughed at them;
Then shut them up in his eternal song,
Well pleased that he had power to do this much.

And meanwhile this poor tangle
Where the weeping and the wailing still goes on,
This endless fraud and shadow
Which has the name of life and is so base, —
All this didst thou despise! Thy sacred muse
Explored the depths of all the universe.
Following the good gentile Philosopher
Who placed thee in the midst of secret things,
Thou didst desire to see as angels see
There where there is no intervening veil;
And thou wouldst love as they do love in heaven.
Up through the ways of love
The humble creature
Pushing his way to the Creator's presence,
Wished to find rest in that eternal Truth
Which taught thee the great love and the great thought.
Here Virgil failed thee,
And thou, deserted,
A lonely human spirit as if drowned
Within the abyss of thy immense desire,
Didst vanish overwhelmed in doubt, —

When as on wings
Angelical there came unto thy grief
She who is love and light and vision
Between the understanding and the True.
No mortal tongue like mine may give her name,
But thou who lovedst didst call her Beatrice.
And so from sphere to sphere
'T was naught but melody that thou didst hear,
'T was naught but one great light that thou didst see,
And every single sense thou hadst was love,
And verse and spirit made one harmony

Like unto her who there revealed herself.
Alas! what caredst thou then
For thy poor country and the endless strife
That rent its cities like, alas! even those
That make forever dark the vales of hell!
From heaven descending thou didst thrice bring down
The Hymn Supreme, and all the while there shone
Upon thy brow a radiance divine
Like his who spake with God in Sinai.

Before thee shining
In all the splendour of the holy Kingdom
Flashed in its crimson light the mortal field
Of Montaperto, and along the wastes
Deserted and malignant came the sound,
Dreary and dull, of dying warriors' sighs:
To which far off responded
With a great cry of mingled human woe
The cursed battle-field of Campaldino.
And thou, Rea Meloria,
Didst rise from the Tuscan sea
To tell the glory of this horrid slaughter,
And of the Thyrrenian shores made desolate
With this our madness, and the sea's great bosom
All stained with blood, and far Liguria's strand
Filled with the moan of lonely Pisan exiles
And children born for fratricidal war.

. . . .

JUVENILIA.

XXXIV

ON THE SIXTH CENTENARY OF DANTE

I saw him, from the uncovered tomb uplifting
His mighty form, the imperial prophet stand.
Then shook the Adrian shore, and all the land
Italia trembled as at an earthquake drifting.

Like morning mist from purest ether sifting,
It marched along the Apenninian strand,
Glancing adown the vales on either hand,
Then vanished like the dawn to daylight shifting.

Meanwhile in earthly hearts a fear did rise,
The awful presence of a god discerning,
To which no mortal dared to lift the eyes.
But where, beyond the gates, the sun is burning,
The races dead of warlike men and wise
With joy saluted the great soul's returning.

LEVIA GRAVIA.

XXXV

BEATRICE

The shining face
Smiled straight into the skies;
A rosy glow was on her archéd neck;

Her radiant brow,
Lofty, serene, and fair,
And her glance like a rose new-blown,

And the fresh smile
Of pure youth,
Awakened in the heart new ecstasies:

But awe-inspiring
And with fear entrancing
Was her presence.

Floating on the wind
In the morning air
Was her sky-blue mantle, her white veil.

Like Our Lady from heaven
She passed before me,
An angel in seeming and yet all so ardent.

My mind stopped thinking
But to look at her,
And the soul was at rest—but for sighing.

Then said I: O how or when
Did earth deserve
That such a mark of love be given her?

What reckless ancestors
Gave thee to the world?
What age ever bore so fair a thing as thou?

What serener star
Produced thy form?
What love divine evolved thee from its light?

Easily the ways of man
Following the blessed guidance

Of thee, Beatrice, were all made new!

—"Not a woman, but the Idea
Am I, which heaven did offer
For man to study when seeking things on high.

"When hearts, not wholly cooled
Of their potential fires,
Fought hard with life severe, and with the truth,

"And to the valiant thinking
And courageous hope
Faith and true love lent arms of constancy,—

"Then, from my airy seat descending,
Among these gallant souls I came,
Kindled and kept alive their ardent zeal;

"And, faithful to my champions,
Clasped in their mighty embrace,
I made them worship Death—yea, and Defeat,

"While, traced by dreamy souls
In verse and colours,
I wandered through the laurels on Arno's banks.

"In vain you look for me
'Mong your poor household gods—
No Bice Portinari—I am the Idea!"

Juvenilia.

XXXVI

"A QUESTI DÍ PRIMA IO LA VIDI. USCIA"

These were the days when first I saw her growing
Like bud to flower in the time of spring,
Her figure such a sweet and lovely thing
As if one heard love's richest music flowing.

The bashful blushes on her cheeks were showing
What native grace her gentle speech could bring;
As on smooth seas the stars their radiance fling,
So in her laughing eyes the soul was glowing.

'T was such I saw her. Now with mad desire
As in a world of stifling air alone
I wander, weak and worn with my inquiring,

Till strength remains only her name to moan
As with each breath I feel my life expiring:
O Light of all my years, where art thou flown?

. . . .

JUVENILIA.

XXXVII

"NON SON QUELL'IO CHE GIÀ D'AMICHE CENE"

I am not he who amid wine cups flowing
Rouses to joy the festive board of friends:
Heavy with bitter weariness is going
The time that to my mind no banquet sends.

Anger alone is that fierce life bestowing
Over whose board my heart all ravenous bends.
O fair green years when brightest hopes were growing
That now lie withered as when summer ends!

Even the charm of sweet imagination
No more its soul-beguiling power retains,
But in its place stands life, mute, dread, appalling,
And over all a shade whose intonation
As if of grief that it alone remains
To some still shore afar is ever calling.

. . . .

Juvenilia.

XXXVIII

THE ANCIENT TUSCAN POETRY

A child in gardens, fields, and city squares
I grew 'mid war's alarms and love's alluring;
But manhood's school of mysteries and cares
Enticed me to the temple's dark immuring.

Where now the lofty dames, with glance securing
What free-born knight or brave civilian dares?
Bright April days the roses bloom assuring?
The oak that through the castle rampart stares?

Poor and alone, again to that dear dwelling
I come where pious love did once deny
That I should heed the Enchantress' sweet impelling.
Open! O Child: though be the times awry,
Thy vision, Beatrice, wakes my heart's rebelling,—
Open! The Tuscan poesy am I!

Levia Gravia.

XXXIX

OLD FIGURINES

Like as an infant, beaten by its mother
or but half conquered in a wayward quarrel,
tired, falls asleep, with its little fists
tight clenched and with tear-wet eyelids, —

So does my passion, O fair Lalage,
sleep in my bosom; nor thinking, nor caring,
whether in rosy May-time wander playing
the other happy infants in the sun.

O wake 't not, Lalage! or thou shalt hear
my passion, like a very God of battles,
putting an end to sports so innocent,
to flay the very heavens with its raging!

Odi Barbare.

XL

MADRIGAL

Breaking his way through the white clouds in the azure,
The sun laughs out and cries:
"O Springtime, come!"

Across the greening hills with placid murmurs
The streams sing back to the breeze:
"O Springtime, come!"

"O Springtime, come!" to his heart the poet is saying,
While gazing, O pure Lalage, in thine eyes!

ODI BARBARE.

XLI

SNOWED UNDER

Slowly the snow-flakes fall through the ashen heavens: no clamour
nor sound whatever comes up from the street.

No cry of the vender of fruits, no rumbling of cart-wheels,
no ballad of love wailing forth from the lips of youth.

Hoarse from the towers of the square the hours groan out,—
Sighs that come from a world far remote from our daylight.

Birds, that homeless wander, peck at the darkened window:
Souls of the lost ones returning! they watch me and call me to them.

Shortly, O dear Ones, shortly—Heart! tame thy restless rebelling—
down to your silence, down to your peaceful shades will I come!

Odi Barbare.

Lector House believes that a society develops through a two-fold approach of continuous learning and adaptation, which is derived from the study of classic literary works spread across the historic timeline of literature records. Therefore, we aim at reviving, repairing and redeveloping all those inaccessible or damaged but historically as well as culturally important literature across subjects so that the future generations may have an opportunity to study and learn from past works to embark upon a journey of creating a better future.

This book is a result of an effort made by Lector House towards making a contribution to the preservation and repair of original ancient works which might hold historical significance to the approach of continuous learning across subjects.

HAPPY READING & LEARNING!

LECTOR HOUSE LLP
E-MAIL: lectorpublishing@gmail.com